A NEW APPROACH TO STAMP COLLECTING

Some rare British stamps dating from 1840 to 1910

PLATE I

A
New
Approach
to

STAMP

COLLECTING

Michael Harrison and Douglas Armstrong

LONDON: B. T. BATSFORD LTD.

First Published, 1953

MADE AND PRINTED IN GREAT BRITAIN BY
WILLIAM CLOWES AND SONS, LIMITED, LONDON AND BECCLES
FOR THE PUBLISHERS
B. T. BATSFORD LTD
4 FITZHARDINGE STREET, PORTMAN SQUARE
LONDON, W.1

PREFACE

AMONG collecting pursuits, Stamp Collecting boasts by far the largest following.

Why do people collect stamps? What is the mysterious urge that impels millions of ordinary citizens the world over to expend time, money and effort upon the ceaseless pursuit of these precious pieces of paper—wherein does their fascination lie? This book is concerned with the why and wherefore of Stamp Collecting. It sets forth and considers the undertones of Modern Philately (which is the pseudo-scientific designation applied to the intensive cult of the postage stamp), social, cultural, political and economic, that have resulted in the rise and development of the hobby, from its beginnings down to the present day.

It is not just another Stamp Book, for it treats neither of Stamp Collecting in general nor of stamps in particular, but of Philately in its relation to the social structure. The authors hold that Stamp Collecting, no less than other manifestations of human interest, reflects the origins, tendencies and aspirations of the human spirit. Such a book is addressed to the stamp-collector-to-be, rather than the already converted lover of stamps. In it an attempt has been made to show that there is something in this thing called Stamp Collecting, after all. We have not assumed the reader has a collection of stamps as yet, nor anything more than an academic interest in the pursuit. We have not set out to write a text-book of "How to Collect Stamps" (that has been done many times already), nor to analyse the nature of the Stamp itself. Our book, then, is in five parts, historical, economic, philosophical, anecdotal and, lastly, artistic; presenting stamps, their background and their significance in the world of to-day.

What we have done is to examine certain aspects of Stamp

7

Collecting against the background of common human activity, of which the issuing and study of stamps are but two manifestations. For those who already collect stamps it may serve, possibly, to widen the purely philatelic outlook and to align Stamp Collecting with world economy and the radical social transformation now taking place in our midst.

DOUGLAS ARMSTRONG
MICHAEL HARRISON

London 1953

CONTENTS

LIST OF ILLUSTRATIONS

ACKNOWLEDGMENT

THE Authors and Publishers wish to thank the following firms for the loan of material for illustrating this book:
Messrs. Frank Godden Ltd., 110 Strand, London W.C.2, for the loan of stamps; Messrs H. R. Harmer Ltd., 41 New Bond street, London W.1, for the loan of colour blocks and photographs; Messrs. Robson Lowe Ltd., 50 Pall Mall, London S.W.1., for the loan of colour blocks.

CHAPTER I

Stamp Collecting in Evolution

ON May 6th, 1840, the world's first adhesive postage stamps were put on sale throughout the post offices of Great Britain. In the guise of a slight convenience, a force destined to have far-reaching commercial, social and political consequences was introduced to mankind through the agency of Her Britannic Majesty's Postmaster-General. Like most notable innovations which have materially altered the pattern of living, the adhesive postage label was rather the combination of two old-established practices than a brand-new idea. Nor was the postage stamp the sole invention of Sir Rowland Hill, as is so often erroneously claimed.

The collecting, carrying and delivery of letters at regular times and for a uniform fee was, in fact, no novelty when the "Penny Black" and "Twopenny Blue" stamps were first offered to the British public.

Nevertheless the Sixth of May, Eighteen-Forty, is the official birthday of the postage stamp as we know it. We shall see how, during more than a century of existence, it has acquired a value in our world surely undreamt of by Sir Rowland Hill and his associates, even in their most optimistic visions.

In the beginning stamp collecting was very much of a go-as-you-please affair. A hundred years ago the adhesive postage label was sufficient of a novelty to ensure that it would be collected and preserved by the acquisitive-minded. Its early collectors were, however, mere accumulators, gathering together such unconsidered trifles in large numbers and putting them to all manner of fanciful uses, such as decorating screens, covering china plates and similar bric-à-brac and even papering whole rooms. In this fashion numbers of the earlier stamp issues have been handed down to posterity. A classic example

15

is an entire sheet of the rare 3-pfennig stamp of Saxony (1850)
(Pl. IV) which, preserved under glass, served for long as a fire-
screen in a nobleman's house until its value was recognised
by a stamp collector. Then there was the famous "stamp
room", in an old Sussex inn, the walls of which were covered
with thousands of stamps of all kinds. Eventually this remarkable wallpaper was bought by a stamp dealer in its entirety
and carefully removed for the sake of a few scarce items. But
this form of stamp collecting had little in common with the
highly specialised and cultured pursuit that it was later to
become. Not until the early sixties of the last century did the
collecting of stamps begin to follow any particular pattern. By
then there were, perhaps, a hundred stamps of all nations to
be acquired and for their reception special albums began to
be designed by Oppen, Lallier and the like. Collections stuck
down in these pioneer albums are still much sought after,
though frequently, alas, their contents turn out to be of a
much later and inferior vintage. Tentative lists of varieties
known to exist, precursors of the cyclopædic stamp catalogues
of to-day, were drawn up by Booty, Mount Brown and Dr.
Grey; the first journal entirely devoted to the hobby, the
Stamp Collectors' Magazine, was published at Bath in 1863;
dealers in postage stamps for collectors were established in
London, Plymouth, Bath, Southampton and elsewhere; an
open-air stamp exchange flourished in Birchin Lane,
London—stamp collecting had come to stay.

The belief is commonly held that stamp collecting started
as a schoolboy's whim. On the contrary its earliest devotees
were to be found among men of science and letters, notably
Sir Daniel Cooper, Dr. J. E. Gray (of the British Museum),
Judge Philbrick and a host of others, including the Rev. J. E.
Stainforth (perpetual Curate of All Hallow's, Staining), whose
Saturday-afternoon *conversaziones* laid the foundations of
what was, in later years, to be known as the Royal Philatelic
Society, London.

By now stamps had acquired a definite, though modest,
value and a regular market in them was springing up. Prices
generally were reckoned in pence or shillings. A pound was

PLATE II

Robson Lowe Ltd.

Uncommon stamps from the Virgin Islands

(*left*) Some valuable British
stamps, worth
about £500

(*below*) A collection of rare
"pence Ceylons"
in fine condition

Robson Lowe Ltd.

Robson Lowe Ltd.

a high figure to pay for a single specimen, and it was not until the first auction sale of postage stamps was held by Sotheby's some years later that the then record sum of £5 was realised.

As time went by and the number of postage stamps to be collected increased, the catalogues and albums grew more and more elaborate. With the introduction of perforations as a means of separating sheets of stamps a fresh complication was introduced. For a while collectors were disinclined to differentiate between stamps that were perforated and those that were not. Many, in fact, trimmed off the scalloped edges with scissors to make them fit into the spaces arbitrarily ruled off in their albums. The discovery of the Parisian *savant*, Dr. Legrand, that stamp perforations varied according to the number of holes punched along the sides of the labels and his invention of a standard gauge for measuring them may be regarded as the first step in the application of scientific methods to the collection of stamps.

From this point serious collectors of stamps were not content with a single example, but must have one with and one without perforations, wherever such existed, and, if more than one machine had been employed, then a sample of each gauge. Thus perforations came to play an important part in the intensive study and collection of stamps, which was then gradually becoming known as *Philately*.

This aspect of stamp collecting gained fresh impetus as philatelists turned their attention to the study of methods of printing and engraving involved in the production of stamps, of the makes and grades of papers upon which they were impressed, the watermarks to be found in their texture and the oft varying shades of ink resulting from the sequence of printings. These and other developments in methods of collecting turned the stamp album from a glorified form of scrap-book into a volume of comprehensive record and absorbing interest.

For the first fifty years it was possible for the collector endowed with patience, perseverance and a reasonably well-filled purse to acquire a fairly complete collection of all stamps issued throughout the world up to that date. The important collection formed by Mr. T. K. Tapling, M.P., and bequeathed by him to the Nation, stops short at the year 1890 and contains at least one specimen of almost all stamps then known to exist. His contemporary, the late Count Ferrari, who continued his collection well into the present century, was even more complete, for he owned the only known copy of the unique 1-cent stamp of British Guiana, 1856, the most valuable stamp in the world.

Most stamp collections of this period were built up on general lines, embracing stamps of all nations with or without their varieties of paper, perforation, colour and printing. Planned and illustrated albums provided spaces for one stamp of each kind, according to the catalogue. But already the total number of stamps to be collected was running well into five figures and the cry was "still they come".

The turn of the century brought with it, in consequence, several innovations in stamp-collecting techniques. As a first step towards limitation collectors began to divide the world of stamps into geographical groups, Europe and the British Empire having the largest followings. Further sub-divisions followed, such as the Australian States, British Africa, North America and so forth. Side by side with this tendency to concentrate upon the postal issues of a few selected countries developed the practice of collecting not by single stamps alone but also in unsevered pairs, blocks of four and even entire sheets as sold by the post offices. Stamps preserved on the original letters were also sought after, where hitherto it had been the invariable custom to remove them from the envelopes. So hard to come by did these collectors' pieces prove that they soon attained a premium over the normal stamps. Aided by such eclectic items advanced collectors were able to reconstruct in part, at least, the histories of successive stamp issues, the methods by which they were printed, make-up of the printing plates, periods of currency, the postage rates that each different value denoted and a hundred and one details of their inception and use, after the manner of the scientist reconstructing a Dinosaur from a single bone. And so was born that, to-day, almost universal phase of Philately known as "specialisation".

From group collecting the next stage in philatelic progression was naturally the collection of stamps of one country upon a still more intensified scale. In the very apt definition of an American writer the trend was towards collecting "everything of something, rather than something of everything". A notable instance of single-country collecting occurred at the time of the Boer War, when a coterie of serious philatelists concentrated their attention upon the rather complicated, and on the whole somewhat unprepossessing, stamps issued by the Transvaal, Colony and Republic. Unfortunately, like many over-zealous pioneers, they over-did it, carrying their researches to such extremes that the general body of collectors has ever since looked askance at what is in fact an historically interesting and philatelically fascinating sequence of stamps. Much the same may be said, though happily in a lesser degree, of the early issues of New South Wales, South Australia, New Zealand, Shanghai, Portuguese India and certain other countries that present to-day over-elaborated lists of varieties in the catalogue. These were but the birth pangs of philatelic specialisation and in due course more rational counsels prevailed. The stamp specialist of to-day is disposed to open his album pages only to pieces that have a positive contribution to make to the record of the stamp issue concerned.

A still more advanced form of Philately made its début in the first decade of the twentieth century in the guise of "single-issue specialisation", which in some cases is further narrowed down to a single stamp. This manifested itself primarily in the side-line of "plating": that is to say, an attempt to reconstruct from single specimens, pairs, strips and blocks a full sheet of stamps as it was originally printed. A first and obvious candidate for study along these lines was the "Penny Black" stamp of Great Britain, with its alphabetical check-letters in the lower corners. In this way many thousands of copies were taken off the market and absorbed into collections, with the result that what was once a stamp in reasonable supply has been forced up to an artificial value out of all proportion to its actual scarcity. Almost all line-engraved

2

British stamps, as well as those of the United States and some other countries, have attracted the attention of philatelic "platers". Needless to say, however, it is only to the more studious type of collector that this aspect of the cult appeals.

Meanwhile the passing of Queen Victoria, and the succession of King Edward VII, opened up a new era so far as the stamps of the British Empire were concerned. Conservative collectors of the old school decided to close their albums with the last of the Victorian issues; the more progressive essayed to "get in on the ground floor" by commencing their collections with the initial issues of the Edwardian era. Their acumen was soon rewarded with a change in the watermark of the British Colonial stamps from a Single to a Multiple Crown and CA device. This quickly rendered obsolete all the earlier printings and sent their values soaring. Ten years after, the change-over from the head of the late King Edward to that of King George V on the Empire's postal issues enabled yet another generation of stamp collectors to start from scratch, as it were; whilst but a short time ago something like three-fifths of the collectors in the United Kingdom favoured first the Commonwealth stamps of the reign of King George VI (Pl. XII) (Pl. IX). To-day we stand upon the threshold of another era in British and Commonwealth stamps, when philatelic history is likely to repeat itself.

Most people would rightly regard the ubiquitous postage label as an emblem of peace and progress and of the comity of nations. Nevertheless stamps have been associated to a remarkable extent with "wars, and rumours of wars". The two world wars in particular both brought in their train a formidable array of special issues arising out of territorial conquest and occupation, the work of the Red Cross and other wartime organisations, that are assiduously collected in a class by themselves under the category of "war stamps".

Between the wars the rise and development of the air-post service evolved another novel branch of Philately that continues to flourish side by side with the more universal cult of the postal adhesive, known as "air-mail collecting". Recent years have brought to the fore, also, yet another school of philatelists who are concerned with the study of stamps in their relation to the history of the Post Office. In their conception the adhesive stamp is merely an incidental attribute of the postal service, their interests extending backward through the ages to embrace all manner of hand-struck postmarks and *cachets* indicating payment of postage, the which they hold, not unreasonably, to be the forerunners of the postage stamp as we know it. So considerable a vogue has this branch of Philately attained that it is the fashion for specialised collections of stamps to be prefaced by a selection of what are commonly termed "pre-stamp covers".

But to collect stamps for pleasure and profit is not necessarily a semi-scientific or highbrow pursuit. The gradual substitution during the present century of pictorial subjects for the numismatically inspired and stereotyped heads of rulers and coats of arms that provided wellnigh exclusively the stamp designs of former days has opened up a wider and more catholic field in the "thematic collection"; of which more anon.

Nor is it the means and methods of collecting alone that have altered with the years. Gone for ever are the vast unfillable spaces of the old-time printed album that no one was ever known to complete. The loose-leaf album of to-day, with its pages neatly ruled in a faint *quadrille* pattern, invites the collector to enshrine those specimens and those alone that are nearest to his heart's desire; and the rest can go hang.

Thus, in rather less than a hundred years, the cycle of stamp collecting has turned full circle. Once more the collecting of stamps is free and unfettered by irksome rules and restrictions and regulated alone by human interests and the personal predilection of the individual collector.

CHAPTER II

The New Stamp Collecting

STAMP COLLECTING has been aptly dubbed "the hobby of a hundred interests". There is something in it to interest everyone. Scarce a phase or aspect of human interest and activity that a collection of stamps does not embrace. Stamps cover by design or association an exceedingly wide range of subjects. Something about a foreign stamp stirs the imagination and finds a responsive chord in almost every intelligent mind. For one thing it is always up to date. New stamps are being issued somewhere nearly every day. In many cases they are bound up with world events in such a way that the stamp album becomes a commentary upon the news of the day. Though stamps are more than a hundred years old, they are never back numbers. Stamp collecting is essentially a "live" hobby.

A popular form of stamp collecting to-day is the thematic or subject collection. As a philatelic side-line it has made, undoubtedly, enormous strides in recent years. Here attention is focused, first and foremost, upon the subject of the stamp design, rather than upon its more strictly philatelic aspect, and calls for no particular technical knowledge. The scope of the modern stamp artist is unbounded, and among the subjects of the countless beautiful and intriguing stamp designs produced nowadays there is something to appeal to almost every taste. Stamps showing ships, aeroplanes, trains, birds, beasts and fishes, ancient monuments, modern architecture and a thousand and one other objects of human interest can be collected according to individual choice and predilection—and a most fascinating and satisfying form of collection they make. The doctor, the sportsman, the farmer, the aviator, the engineer, the book-lover, the musician or the actor, "the butcher, the baker, the candlestick-maker", and a score of

PLATE III

SHIPS ILLUSTRATED ON STAMPS

A Solomon Islands canoe; "guffahs" on the Tigris; the Greek cruiser *Averoff*; "gyassas" on the Nile; seventeenth-century ship *Olive Blossom*; the Imperial German Yacht *Hohenzollern*; Adenese dhow; the Royal Yacht *Britannia*; a cargo steamer; a Malayan "proa"; American yacht *Lucie*; Colombus's flagship; H.M.S. *Bounty*; a liner and a junk

PLATE IV

"Woodblock" Cape; "Twelvepence" Canada; unique One Cent British Guiana, 1856; "Connell" stamp of New Brunswick; U.S.A. "inverted flags"; Principality of Trinidad; Three Pfennig Saxony; stamp of Sedang; Serbian "Death Mask" stamp; Two Cents British Guiana, 1850; type-written stamps of Uganda other trades and professions may acquire just those stamps that appeal to them most strongly in association with their work or play. The attraction lies, not in the minutiæ of engraving, printing and paper-making, but in the recognition and classification of the types of ships and aircraft, the genus of animals or the lives and achievements of the personalities who have been honoured by grateful countries with their portraits on stamps. "In short, sir, fancy what you most affect."

The vogue may be said to have started with "Animal Stamps". Until the advent of the first wholly pictorial series of stamps, emanating from the State of North Borneo in the year 1894, the only animals depicted on stamps had been the symbolical Beaver of Canada, the Llama of Peru, and of course the heraldic Eagles of Austria, Germany, the United States, etc. The new set from North Borneo, however, included such examples of indigenous fauna as the "Roussa" stag, the Argus pheasant and an alligator, later to be joined by the orang-outang and the honey-bear, in their native haunts. Since then almost every form of animal life, wild and domestic, has been the subject of stamp designs the world over. So it came about that a "Stamp Zoo" became the forerunner of the many types of thematic collections now prevailing. Some collectors may recall the time when as a "stunt" a stamp shop in the Strand displayed a whole series of animal stamps in miniature cages, like a menagerie.

After animals came ships. Almost every type of craft that has sailed the seven seas, from the coracle-like "guffas" of Iraq to the transatlantic liners *Normandie* and *Neiuw Amsterdam*, have been introduced into the designs of the world's postage stamps, and it must not be forgotten that the rarest stamp in the world, with its crude "cut" of a sailing brig, is itself a "Ship Stamp".

"Sporting Stamps" present another very attractive field of thematic stamp collecting that has a world-wide following. The creation of special stamps as a contribution towards the cost of the revival of the Olympic Games, at Athens in 1896, has been followed by the majority of subsequent meetings, including that held in London in 1948. A wide range of sports and outdoor pastimes from ski-ing to horse-racing are embraced in the ever-growing number of stamps associated with sport, to the extent that a special catalogue of them has been published in Italy, where an exhibition devoted entirely to this aspect of stamp collecting was lately held. This form of collecting lends itself admirably to descriptive "writing-up" of the pages, the stamps themselves serving to illustrate the theme, and therein lies one of its chiefest charms. To the philatelist "the stamp's the thing", but with the thematic stamp collector it is the subject that comes first. That is not to say that philatelic practices and principles cannot and should not be applied to a thematic collection. Indeed, it is both practical and desirable that the annotation should embrace such matters as the method of production, names of artists, engravers and printers (when available), paper, watermark and similar philatelic information, not forgetting, of course, the date of issue. There is no reason whatever why the two schools of stamp collecting should not flourish side by side, without any question of rivalry.

The field of thematic collecting is almost limitless in its scope. Among the subjects represented at a recent exhibition were: Famous People; Botany; Saints and Martyrs; Horticulture; Dancing; Horse-Racing; Music and Musicians; Mountains, Lakes and Rivers; Waterfalls; the Red Cross, etc. We know of collections devoted to "Pin-up Girls", "Wine, Woman and Song", and one particularly ingenious effort in the shape of a "Life Story of the Owner", his birthplace, the school where he was educated, his employment, military service, places visited, in fact an autobiography in stamps.

Variations on the theme are almost inexhaustible, as has already been indicated. The list that follows is by no means complete, though it may possibly assist collectors in making their selections:

ARCHITECTURE: Buildings, ancient and modern, from the Parthenon to the latest achievements of Soviet architects, adorn the stamps of a wide range of countries.

ARCHÆOLOGY: The ruined cities of Greece, Crete, Carthage,

Ankor, Palmyra, as well as relics of the Maya civilisation, are among the many subjects of interest to the archæologist that have been drawn upon by stamp designers.

ASTRONOMY: Galileo and Copernicus have been immortalised on stamps of Italy and Poland respectively. The "Southern Cross" figures on a variety of stamps from Brazil and Australia, whilst a solar eclipse, the spiral galaxy of the "Hunting Dog" and the extra-galactic nebula in Virgo are a few of the subjects that go to the making of a collection of "Astronomical Stamps".

ART: The Art of the postage stamp is a modern art, reflecting to some extent the trend of national delineation and design. In this respect stamp designs and motives present fascinating study. Furthermore, a number of the masterpieces of eminent artists like Rubens, Rembrandt, Van Dyck, Holbein, Michelangelo, da Vinci, Della Robbia and others have been reproduced in miniature in the space of a postage stamp. Here is a wide and fertile field for the artistically inclined.

AUTOGRAPHS: The autograph-hunter will find quite a number of stamps bearing reproductions of the signatures of the famous, Ibsen and Tolstoi among them.

AVIATION: The rise and development of aviation through the centuries has been a favourite theme with modern stamp artists. Italy has thus honoured the memory of Leonardo da Vinci; Brazil, Father Bartolomeo de Gusmao and his aerostat. Santos Dumont, the Wright brothers and other pioneers of the air also appear with their primitive air-craft on the stamps of the nations. Aeroplanes of every description and period are to be found on the special stamps issued for air-mail purposes in all parts of the world. Famous flights by Hawker, Alcock and Brown, Ross Smith, De Pinedo, Lindbergh and Count von Zeppelin are all recorded in a collection of air stamps that constitutes a lasting memorial to their prowess.

BIRD-LIFE: Birds of every kind, from the South American condor, to the turtle-dove of Japan, go to make up a veritable philatelic aviary well calculated to fascinate any bird-lover. Particularly noteworthy is the series of African birds pictured on the stamps of Portuguese Angola in 1951.

BIG GAME: The big-game hunter will find his quarry upon a host of stamps picturing lion, tiger, elephant, rhino, giraffe, bison, antelope, bear and other hunted animals from Africa to the Amazon.

BIOGRAPHY: Stamp biographies of famous men and women have emanated from Russia (Tolstoi, Chekov, Stefan Razin, Rimski-Korsakov, etc.), Portugal (Camoens, Castel Branco, Vasco da Gama, etc.), Spain (Goya, Cervantes) and a score of other nations, including a whole gallery of American Presidents.

BATTLES: Famous battles by land and sea that have inspired stamp pictures include Navarino Bay (Greece), Rolica (Portugal), Yorktown (U.S.A.) and Sarandi (Uruguay).

BRIDGES: The great bridge spanning Sydney Harbour heads a whole series of similar structures culminating in the good-will bridge over the Uruguay River that links Argentina and Brazil.

CHARITY: Postage stamps serve to-day many purposes beside that for which they were first intended. One of them is the collecting of small doles on behalf of charitable organisations, on a national scale. Charity-cum-postage stamps come principally from Continental countries, an outstanding example being the annual issues made each Yuletide in Switzerland in the interests of the child-welfare institution "Pro-Juventute".

CURRENCY AND COINS: The postage stamp being in itself a form of currency there is a close affinity between Philately and Numismatics. In the United States banknotes of small denominations were actually printed from stamp dies. There, too, and in certain other countries stamps encased in mica were used as emergency coinage. Coins of ancient Greece, together with those of newer vintage, have furnished the designs of a variety of stamps. The beautiful head of Queen Victoria which graced the first stamps of all was derived from a medal made by the eminent engraver William Wyon.

CYCLING: A small but interesting group of stamps is concerned with special delivery of mails by cyclist messengers, both of the old "push-bike" and the motor-cycle eras. One of the most historical of these "cyclist" stamps was printed by photography during the Siege of Mafeking for franking letters sent by bicycle post within the defences.

DOGS: Dog-lovers will find a fair sprinkling of canine subjects on stamps, among them Landseer's famous head of a Newfoundland dog upon a ½-cent stamp of Britain's oldest colony. A later issue shows the mascot of the Royal Newfoundland Regiment. Most striking of all, however, is a charge of war-dogs which accompanied the cavalry at the Battle of Sarandi, as shown on the commemorative stamps emanating from Uruguay on the centenary of the engagement, in 1925.

EGYPTOLOGY: The golden mask of Tut-ankh-Amen, the statue of Rameses II, the head of Queen Nefertiti and bas-reliefs from the Nile temples are among the objects of interest to Egyptologists that have been reproduced upon the postage stamps of that country.

ELECTRICITY: The story of electrical power, from the experiments of Volta, Gramme, Popov, Edison and Graham Bell to the hydro-electric schemes of the Shannon and the Dnieper, is told in stamps of many lands, that "he who runs may read".

ENGINEERING: Engineering wonders of the world, such as the Panama Canal, the Assuan Dam and the Trans-Andean Railway, are perpetuated by issues of commemorative stamps that hold a special appeal for engineers the world over.

ETHNOLOGY: Those who hold, with Pope, that the "proper study of mankind is Man" will find a wealth of material in the numerous types and species of the human race that are to be found on the world's postage stamps. In many cases they are represented in their native haunts or arrayed in characteristic national or regional costume, thus adding further to their interest and attraction.

EXPLORATION: Columbus, Cabot, Vasco da Gama, Tasman, Cook, Sturt and Stanley are but a few of the great explorers of the earth whose name and fame are handed down to posterity on stamps.

FARMING: Farming in many lands, from the golden prairies of Canada to the paddy-fields of Borneo, offers yet another absorbing field for a thematic stamp collection calculated to arrest the attention of agriculturalists.

FISHES AND FISHERY: The cod-fish is Newfoundland's "currency" and as such finds place appropriately upon several of her stamps. New Zealand sends the game sword-fish, and Liberia the unique bommi-fish. Salmon-fishing with rod and line and the more primitive fishing with torch and spear by natives of the Fiji Islands are subjects to fascinate the angler. The Portuguese territory of Mozambique produced in 1951 a striking series of stamps showing almost every known species of fish found in African waters.

FLAGS: Not a few countries have chosen their national flags to appear on their stamps. Argentina had a special issue to mark the centenary of the creation of her "Bandera Nacional". Flags of the twenty-one Pan-American nations are incorporated in the designs of a number of stamps issued in 1940 in honour of the fiftieth anniversary of the Union.

FLOWERS, TREES AND SHRUBS: Horticulture in its many aspects has been laid under heavy contribution by artists responsible for the world's stamps. The flowers, trees and shrubs depicted on stamps form a botanical garden in miniature. They range from the exotic orchids of Colombia (South America), to the English rose and the lilies of France; from the blue gums of Australia to the cedars of Lebanon.

HISTORY: Philately has been aptly dubbed "the handmaiden of History". The stories of many nations may be traced in their stamps: France, as Empire and Republic, the rise and fall of the German Reich, the growth of the Soviet Union, Italy in union and disunion. Philately and politics walk oft-times hand in hand and there is a wealth of material for the historian and the archivist in the history of our times as it unfolds itself through the changing faces of the world's postage stamps.

HERALDRY: Coats of arms and heraldic devices of various kinds have been adopted, as an alternative to portraiture, for the stamps of countless countries, Great Britain and the Empire not excepted. Properly annotated with explanatory notes they make a most interesting and instructive collection for those who delight in the ancient art.

HORSES AND HORSEMEN: One of the most remarkable action

pictures to be represented upon a stamp is that of a Moorish horseman riding his Arab steed at full gallop across the desert waste of Spanish Morocco. The number of equine stamps, however, is not extensive, though recent additions from Germany and Austria are remarkable for the fact that they glorify the racehorse—a most unusual subject for a stamp design.

IMPORTS AND EXPORTS: Commercial propaganda has been widely conducted through the medium of the ubiquitous postage stamp. Products and industries of many lands are publicised on their stamps, giving an insight into world trade.

INDUSTRY: Coalmining, ironfounding, smelting, weaving and printing are a few only of the staple industries that find their place in a collection of "Industrial stamps".

INVENTIONS AND INVENTORS: Inventors whose achievements have been honoured upon the stamps of their native lands include Edison (electric light), Bell (telephone), William Kress (internal-combustion engine), Marconi (wireless), Nobel (explosives) and a host of others. The United States dedicated a whole series of stamps to American inventors in 1940; so did Austria, in 1936.

LAKES: Some of the most beautiful lake scenery in the world may be found in the designs of pictorial stamps from all parts of the globe. New Zealand contributes Lakes Taupo and Wakatipu, Bolivia Lake Titicaca, Switzerland Lake Lugano and many less familiar but no less picturesque sheets of water elsewhere.

LANGUAGES: The number of different languages written on the faces of stamps is almost equal to the number of stamp-issuing countries. Some, indeed, bear more than one language, notably Palestine (English, Hebrew and Arabic), South Africa (English and Afrikaans), Switzerland (French, German and Italian) and so on. The linguist will find an absorbing pastime in the translation of some of the less familiar inscriptions.

LIFESAVING: Famous lighthouses throughout the world find place on the stamps of a limited number of countries, whilst others have for their subject lifeboat institutions and sea-rescue services. All have their particular interest.

LITERATURE: Authors, poets and men of letters generally have been freely honoured by having special stamps dedicated to their memories; a numerous and worthy band. Even the newspaper man has not been forgotten in Pulitzer, founder of the *New York Herald*, whose portrait appears on a recent 3-cent stamp of the United States.

MACHINERY: The machine-minded collector has at his selection a goodly selection of stamps showing machines of various types in operation, from the humble lathe (Russia) to the mechanical harvester (Canada).

MEDICINE: The noble work of the medical and nursing professions has not gone unrecorded on the stamps of the nations. A remarkably interesting collection can be formed of stamps with medical associations, from Hygieia, Goddess of Health, to Dr. Carlos J. Finlay, conqueror of "Yellow Jack".

MINING: The man interested in mining can collect a variety of stamps connected with the mining of coal, gold, emeralds and suchlike spoils of the earth from Colombia, South Africa, Russia, the Saar and other well-known centres of the industry.

MOTORING: The first horseless carriage to be pictured on a stamp was an electric cab, in Washington, on a United States stamp of 1901. Early models of Benz and Daimler motor-cars are the subject of some German stamps of 1939. Many other types of motor-propelled vehicles, including tractors and tanks, are shown on stamps of different countries.

MOUNTAINS AND MOUNTAINEERING: The climber who is philatelically inclined has spread before him a gigantic panorama of most of the world's most famous heights and some that are little known. Austria, Switzerland, South and North America, Persia and Borneo each contribute their quota to this picturesque and awe-inspiring collection.

MYTHOLOGY: Greek, Scandinavian, German, Hindu, Chinese and Japanese mythologies have inspired the artists of those nations to miniature illustrations that retell the familiar folklore and legends in the form of stamps.

MUSIC AND MUSICIANS: One of the finest collections of musical stamps in existence has been formed by Mr. Theodore Steinway of piano fame. One of its highlights is a Polish stamp

PLATE V

RARE MODERN STAMPS

£25 Northern Nigeria (£550); 10s. Malta, watermark Cr.C.A. (£60); 1d. Transvaal, 1905, watermark Anchor (£30); 1-mark Togo Occupation Franco-Anglaise, 1914 (unique); 10s. Great Britain "I.R. OFFICIAL" (£2,000); British Central Africa, 2d. and 4d., watermark Mult.C.A., (£500); Cook Islands, ½d. "centre inverted", (£100)

PLATE VI

SOME RARE AIR-MAIL STAMPS

U.S.A. "inverted centre"; Ross-Smith Flight, London–Australia, 1919; MS. overprint for the Handley-Page flight, 1919; Hawker Trans-Atlantic Air Mail, 1919; De Pinedo flight, Newfoundland–Rome, 1927; "Miss Columbia" Air Mail, Newfoundland–Scilly Isles, 1930 portraying Paderewski and autographed by the master pianist. Chopin, Beethoven, Mozart, Schubert, Rheinberger, Sousa and many more names enshrined in the history of music are preserved in the stamp album, to say nothing of stamps depicting musicians of many lands with their curious, sometimes barbaric instruments.

MAPS: Some really excellent maps have been engraved from time to time in the small space of a postage stamp. They range from the British Empire, on Mercator's projection, to a Spanish reproduction of an ancient chart of the Amazon.

NATURAL HISTORY: Visitors to the Natural History Museum, South Kensington, may have noticed in the entrance a frame containing an assortment of stamps of all nations showing birds, beasts and fishes. The Smithsonian Institute at Washington goes a step further by inserting cards bearing the appropriate stamps, with a detailed description, in the cases alongside the actual specimens on view. A Stamp Zoo is at once one of the most popular and extensive branches of thematic stamp collecting (Pl. XIII).

NAVY: Naval subjects illustrated on stamps embrace Nelson's *Victory*, a Nile gunboat, Liberia's one-ship navy (sunk by the Germans in 1915) and H.M.S. *Achilles* of River Plate renown.

NAVIGATORS: Famous navigators in whose honour special stamps have been issued by their grateful countries include Vasco da Gama, Columbus, Cabot, Prince Henry the Navigator, Cook, Tasman, Magellan, Hudson, Bering and La Perouse, to name only a few whose exploits are inscribed upon the scroll of Philately as well as of History.

OIL: The quest for oil has not failed to leave its mark upon the stamps of the nations. Azerbaijan, Colombia, Surinam, Venezuela and a score of other oil-producing or storing countries have featured the golden stream on their postal issues.

PEACE: Next to war, the blessings of peace have been a favourite subject with modern stamp artists. Inevitably the cessation of hostilities in World Wars I and II brought in its train a plethora of peace stamps of every description. Each time neutral Switzerland was first in the field with a commemorative issue.

POSTS AND POSTMEN: It is natural, perhaps, that the postal service, of which the stamp is itself but a humble servant, should be glorified in the designs of certain special issues of postage stamps. Sweden is one of those countries that have traced the history of their post offices on stamps. France, Bulgaria, Greece and other countries have sold charity postage stamps for the benefit of postal employees.

POETS AND POETRY: Among the galaxy of poets immortalised on the stamps of their own or other countries are Dante, Villon, Goethe, Gertrudis Gomez de Avellaneda, Byron, Longfellow, Kivi and Mayakovski. There are many more.

RAILWAYS: Since the locomotive has played so prominent a part, for many years, in the carriage of the mails, it is not surprising that trains and railways should figure so largely in the philatelic diorama. When a locomotive appeared for the first time on a United States stamp in 1869, a cynic is said to have remarked that it was there to show how Congressmen made money. Seventy-five years later a similar stamp was issued in America to commemorate the anniversary of the completion of the first transcontinental railway, also in 1869.

RED CROSS: Stamps tell the story of the Red Cross from its inception to the end of World War II. Hundreds of stamps coming from all parts of the globe bear witness to its work and have helped to collect funds for the relief of the sick and injured, in war and peace. A collection of Red Cross stamps is surely one of the most inspiring that can be imagined.

RELIGION: Abbeys and churches, priests and prelates, holy pictures and relics, saints and martyrs, even an image of Christ himself, go to the making of a collection of "Religious Stamps". Nor has the Christian faith a monopoly: Mohammedism, Judaism, Buddhism, Shinto, are also represented.

SCIENCE: Prominent among the great men and women of science who have been honoured from time to time upon the stamps of their own or other countries are Pasteur, Curie, Tesla, Lomonsov, Scheele, Reede and Jane Adams, to name only a few. Handsome tribute has, in fact, been paid by those responsible for the issuing and designing of commemorative stamps to science and scientists the world over.

SCOUTING: Stamps dedicated to the Scouting Movement
have been issued by Holland and the Dutch Indies, France,
Roumania, Hungary, Germany and Russia. The founder of
the movement and first Chief Scout, Major-General R. S. S.
Baden-Powell himself, is portrayed on a local stamp issued
during the siege of Mafeking in 1900.

SHIPS AND SHIPPING: (Pl. III) Few subjects have inspired stamp
artists to a greater extent. The first "ship" stamp came from
Trinidad, B.W.I., in 1847. It was printed privately to pre-pay
letters consigned by the coastwise packet-boat *Lady McLeod*.
Almost every known type of craft, from the Roman galley to
the ocean greyhound, is to be found in infinite variety upon
the stamps of the nations. "Ship stamps" are generally one
of the most popular forms of subject collecting.

SPORT AND ATHLETICS: At first there would seem to be little
affinity between such essentially active pursuits as sport
and athletics and the more sedentary occupation of Philately.
Nevertheless the association is closer than might appear.
Many thousands of pounds have, as already mentioned, been
raised for the revival of the Olympic Games through the
medium of special issues of stamps, made in their interests
by almost every country where they have been held, Britain
providing the most recent issue on the occasion of the XIVth
Olympiad. Cricket excepted, almost every outdoor sport and
game is represented in the stamp album, including football,
baseball, basket-ball, lawn tennis and hurley.

TRANSPORTATION: "Transportation is Civilisation" according to Kipling, and but for the civilising influence of modern
methods of communication the carriage of the mails would
have been less speedy than it is to-day. It is fitting, therefore,
that the many and varied means of transport employed in the
service of the post should provide the motives of so large a
number of postage stamps. They range from the Aztec courier
on the express letter stamp of Mexico, through the era of the
stage-coach and sailing-packet to the locomotive, the steamship, the aeroplane and the helicopter; mutely eloquent of postal
progress and the evolution of letter-carrying through the ages.

TRAVEL: "For to admire, and for to see, for to behold this

world so wide" is a common ambition, normally achieved, however, only by those with leisure and means. Yet the stamp collector "with extensive view" can, in fact, "survey mankind from China to Peru" without stirring from the comfort of his hearth and home. The wonders of the world, the scenic splendours, the sights and cities of the two hemispheres are brought home to him through the medium of hundreds of miniature views. The Pyramids, the Kremlin, the Taj Mahal, the Temple of the Tooth, Fujiyama, the Great Wall of China, Popocatepetl, the Victoria Falls, Yellowstone Park and Sydney Harbour pass before his eyes in a glorious panorama when he makes his Grand Tour with stamps.

WAR STAMPS: Wars and rumours of wars have been responsible for a vast number of special stamps issued under naval and military authority. They embrace many minor campaigns as well as the two world wars and some of them are of considerable rarity. The field is a big one, but philatelically and politically full of interest.

WIRELESS: A small but growing group of stamps is associated with the invention and development of wireless communications. Marconi, Popov and other radio pioneers have had stamps issued in their honour, whilst several important wireless stations are pictured on stamps.

WOMEN: Famous women from Joan of Arc to Susan B. Antony are immortalised on their countries' stamps. A whole series of stamps of the British Commonwealth bearing the likeness of Queen Elizabeth II is making its appearance. A feminist stamp collection might well appeal to collectors of the fair sex, the number of whom is not inconsiderable.

*   *   *

And there, dear reader, you have it. "You pays your money, and takes your choice." You may pay much or little, according to your inclination and purse, but your choice is practically limitless.

*   *   *

This, then, may be rightly called THE NEW STAMP COLLECTING. Already societies catering for its devotees have sprung up in America, on the Continent, in Great Britain and as far afield as South Africa. Several of these publish their own bulletins.

Thematic collecting is also developing a literature of its own. Whilst, to some extent, the *Encyclopædia Britannica* is the most practical text-book for the thematic collector, a number of more specialised works are at his disposal. A most comprehensive and informative book on *Zoology in Postage Stamps* is written by Messrs. W. Dennis Way and O. D. Standen, F.Z.S., and there is another excellent work dealing with *Medicine and Stamps*. Handbooks have been published likewise on *Ship Stamps* (Rowland H. Hill), *Native Races of the Stamp Album* (A. E. Gould), and many others.

CHAPTER III

Nationalism in Stamp Collecting

OUT of the impulse for selective stamp collecting that manifested itself in the opening years of the twentieth century there emerged, quite understandably, a nationalistic trend. What more natural than that, faced with the choice of collecting stamps of a particular country or group, the collector's selection should fall upon those of his own, his native land, in preference to all others? So far as British philatelists were concerned the choice was a fairly wide one, for it embraced not only the Mother Country, but the whole of the British Dominions beyond the seas. The French philatelist was in somewhat similar case, for he had at his disposal an almost equally fertile field in the many and varied stamp issues of France's Colonial Empire. German philately ranged from the stamps of the old Thurn and Taxis postal monopoly through the individual issues of the old states and principalities that went to make up Bismarck's German Empire, supplemented by its colonial possessions and postal agencies in foreign parts. Before the Italian stamp collector opened up a wide vista encompassing the pre-union kingdoms and grand duchies of Naples, Sicily, Parma, Tuscany, Sardinia, Modena and the Papal State, through the historic stamps of the House of Savoy, in triumph and disaster, together with those of the newly founded Italian colonies of North Africa and the Red Sea littoral. Spain and Portugal, domestic and colonial, presented like opportunities for philatelic exploitation, to say nothing of Holland, and Belgium with its fledgling colony on the Congo. The field, in fact, was wide in the extreme.

Strange to say, however, it was on the other side of the Atlantic that the national impulse in Philately found its fullest expression. American collectors turned with avidity from the wellnigh hopeless attempt to amass the stamps of the whole world to the more encouraging possibilities offered by the ever-increasing emissions of the United States; so much so, in fact, that nine out of ten collectors in America collect, first and foremost, stamps of the Great Republic, often to the exclusion of all else. The reason for this is not far to seek. From the outset the Post Office Department of the United States has produced postage stamps that in design and execution are second to none. Of intent they have been designed, more especially the more modern issues, to foster the patriotic spirit and promote popular interest in the history and progress of the land of their birth. Moreover their acquisition is made easy by the existence in Washington of a Philatelic Bureau which supplies collectors (and dealers) with all current and many recent issues of United states stamps at "face" value. Since the American Post Office produces special issues of an historical or biographical character at frequent intervals the keen collector can keep his collection up to date at very little cost. Needless to say this applies only to stamps issued within the last twenty years or so. The older and more valuable issues have still to be acquired through the collectors' market. Estimates place the total number of stamp collectors in the United States at round about two millions; and the vast majority of these are America-minded. The accent therefore is on American stamps, in the stamp shops, in the stamp journals and in the stamp societies throughout the United States.

British collectors were slower to adopt a national attitude towards stamp collecting, except in the wider field of the Empire as a whole. The cult of "Colonials" came in towards the end of the 'nineties and rapidly gained ground, but for some little time stamps of the United Kingdom itself were treated as merely incidental to the whole, save for a very small band of enthusiasts who were beginning to explore their potentialities. In the first place this took the form of intensive study of the recess-printed issues from 1840 to 1870, scant regard being paid to the less pleasing though more economical surface-printed series. The changes in printing and design that followed on the accession of King George V brought about a

minor boom in contemporary issues by a modernistic school
of Philately, but for some inexplicable reason what are known
as the "middle issues" of the later Victorian period were to
all intents and purposes passed over. Only within comparatively
recent times have they been sought after to any considerable
extent. That the stamps of Great Britain do attract a substantial following of present-day collectors goes without saying.
They have gained in popularity enormously during recent
years. Nevertheless the proportion of collectors in Great
Britain who specialise in the stamps of their own country is
infinitely less than in the case of our American cousins.

What has been the effect of this restricted form of collecting
upon the body philatelic? On the whole beneficial. Collecting
on the spot, as it were, has obvious advantages. First of all
abundance and availability of material. One is more likely to
find large quantities of, let us say, British stamps in the United
Kingdom than in any other country, and so on. Next, sources
of information. Records and archives, the very existence of
which may be unknown to the collector overseas, are accessible
to the man on the spot. Firms who actually printed the stamps,
or their successors, are at hand to help unravel knotty problems.
The postal authorities can also be consulted; all of which can
be of the greatest possible assistance to the student philatelist.
It is to these factors that philatelists owe the many authorita-
tive text-books, check lists and descriptive catalogues that
have been published on the stamps of particular countries and
colonies. In most instances these have been the co-operative
work of members of local philatelic societies who have been
granted special facilities by the Post Office Department and
have proved of inestimable benefit to collectors of the stamps
concerned.

One snag, from the collector's point of view, is that this
concentrated collecting tends to force up prices against himself. Values of British stamps, for example, have increased as
much as twenty times within almost as many years. Not much
longer ago an average used copy of a "Penny Black" could
be bought freely for a modest shilling—to-day the same specimen would fetch a pound or more. For a great many years

PLATE VII

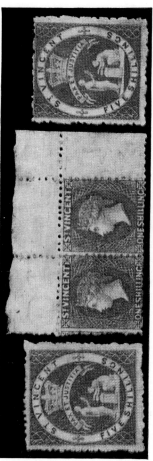

"Collectors' pieces" from St. Vincent,
one of the Windward Islands

Robson Lowe Ltd.

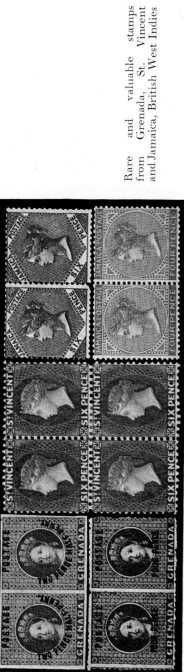

Rare and valuable stamps
from Grenada, St. Vincent
and Jamaica, British West Indies

Robson Lowe Ltd.

the markets of the world have been scoured for American stamps of every kind, all of which have found their way to New York and thence into the albums of American collectors. The result has been that prices have risen consistently and continue to do so. Nationalism causes British stamps to fetch more in Britain, American in the United States, French in France, Dutch in Holland; in fact, with few exceptions, stamps generally are more highly valued in the country of their origin than anywhere else.

CHAPTER IV

The Economics of Stamp Collecting

IT was only during the first few years of stamp collecting that the profit motive was almost disregarded; in fact, it was never entirely overlooked. Amongst the first publications dealing with the hobby were priced catalogues, which, in the light of what has since transpired, make nostalgic reading to-day. The purely material side has more and more prevailed with the passage of time; so much so that the collector who ignores this monetary aspect (he does exist) is in a decidedly small, and admittedly select, minority.

Once it was the fashion to deplore the sordid "money" aspect of Philately, but whether deplorable or not, financial interests have steadily come to the forefront. The cultural side has not suffered because the idea of gain was so often present; in fact, expectancy of profit has been a powerful incentive to research. Many of the enthusiastic amateurs of sixty or seventy years ago—those who did so much original research work in stamps plentiful in their time—were actuated by the hope of profitable discoveries. They were often well rewarded for their industry, and in turn the stamp-collecting public of to-day owes these pioneer philatelists a great deal for putting the hobby on a sound footing. In fact, they lifted stamp collecting out of the ruck of schoolboy hobbies, without so much hair-splitting as some of their successors indulged in.

In its turn, too, the strong and ever-growing financial interest in the hobby has had a tonic effect all round and has been responsible for a powerfully stabilising influence on stamp values, so much so that nowadays there are few sounder securities.

Moreover much publicity has been secured in the lay press as the result of realisations of stamps—mainly in auction. It will be noted that in nearly all articles in the non-philatelic press regarding stamp collecting the financial side is always considered to be of the greatest news value—and is therefore (sometimes unduly) stressed. In the long run this attitude must have its effect on the potential philatelists who read these notes with interest.

Since the early nineteen-twenties, owing to political unrest and various other disturbing causes in different parts of the world, more particularly on the European continent, many currencies have, to say the least, at times lacked stability. Others, though seemingly stable enough, have in many instances been supported by artificial devices of such a nature that the possibility of their collapsing was always present. Therefore the stamp-minded citizens of many European states have been attracted by stamps as being a commodity of international value, not, in their opinion, subject to any serious depreciation in the world market. In this connection it is worthy of note that a very large proportion of the population of many European states are stamp collectors—many of course on a very small scale, which is inevitable when countless thousands of enthusiasts have to be considered.

Stamps, it might be said here, have turned out to be "the goods"—the citizens have been correct in their selection of an investment medium. World upheavals have never depressed the stamp market, except perhaps temporarily; rather have stamp values improved in troublous times; at any rate, in comparison with other forms of investment, the results have consistently proved most favourable.

The strength and importance of stamp auctioneers as well as dealers is apparent to all who read advertisements in the philatelic and even in the lay press. Auctioneering is a branch of the handling of postage stamps, rare and common, old and new, which has been developed to an enormous extent during the past thirty years and has now attained a particularly high degree of efficiency. The combined annual turnover of stamp auctioneers in England must run into some hundreds of thousands of pounds annually—and what is more, seems to be still increasing.

There are, of course, literally thousands of established stamp dealers in England, the United States and the rest of the world. Many are really large organisations with staffs running into three figures or thereabouts, whilst hundreds of others are substantial business concerns turning over annually surprisingly large amounts.

‧Dealers nowadays have almost without exception to specialise in certain classes of stamps to meet the requirements of their customers, who at some time or other nearly always tend to limit the scope of their collections. This specialisation does not necessarily mean that every tiny variety is sought after or even recognised, but more often than not a "limited sectional" collection is embarked upon. This would often be a fitter description than "specialism" in respect of the activities of many philatelists.

The legions of the old-fashioned general collectors have been thinning for many years past, simply because of the utter impossibility of making a respectable showing. The rapidly growing number of stamps, not to mention varieties of those stamps, precludes the possiblity of even approaching completeness, an object which every collector hopes to achieve in some measure. A cursory glance at the catalogue reveals the utter hopelessness of even attempting such a task. A millionaire could not do it without the assistance of secretaries —a good many assistants would be required to arrange and to keep up to date a whole world collection on specialised lines. Even on a simplified basis such a collection is almost out of reach of the individual philatelist who has other preoccupations, and so stamp collecting has, of necessity, been diverted into multifarious channels, each available according to individual tastes and means—and not forgetting the limits of spare time at the collector's disposal. There survives to-day but one important collection in this category. It belongs to a wealthy South African collector, and is said to be only about a score of stamps short of completion, according to catalogue.

The collecting of the older and so-called "classic" issues has always been the backbone of the hobby, but here again changes are taking place—the requirements of the philatelic investor tending more and more to be confined to fine and unusual pieces.

Stamps not especially rare as singles are fetching what seem to be fantastic prices in pairs and more especially in blocks. Instances are so many and so varied, covering old issues, and more recently stamps of the middle period and even comparatively modern varieties, that it would be impossible to mention even a fraction of the number. Experience however, soon teaches those who are interested. An excellent example is to be found in the ever-popular triangular "Capes". The 1s. emerald green (1863–64), catalogued in two shades, is priced at £40 in used condition; a fair price for a good example, though cheap for a really superb, lightly postmarked, good margined example of good colour. A used pair, however, is a great rarity, even in a not-so-brilliant state, and a really superb pair in perfect used state should be worth upwards of £200. Unused pairs and blocks of this popular "Shilling Emerald" also fetch more, *pro rata*, than singles, but not in the same proportion as the used stamps, for at one time these were available in large pieces. Thirty years ago it was possible to buy blocks of these stamps of any size, according to the whim of the purchaser. It was said in those days that these unused "remainders" (as they were then wrongly termed) would never be absorbed, but they have all gone, and it is only when a collection is broken up that these pairs and larger pieces are available.

This is just one example amongst the many imperforate stamps, but of late the demand for blocks of four has extended to perforated issues, and even quite modern stamps fetch a premium when in blocks, in certain instances. This is contrary to the custom of a few years ago when one could often get a reduction when buying a fairly plentiful stamp by taking a large block—a reduction for quantity, as it were.

Stamps comparatively common in themselves but difficult to obtain in perfect mint condition (notably those printed on highly surfaced paper) have been much sought after in recent years, and prices far and away above catalogue quotations are nowadays quite the rule. In blocks, these types of stamps are, of course, particularly scarce in superb mint condition. Other outstanding examples are the "Columbus" issue of the United States of America (1892) and the "Jubilee" issue of Canada (1897) (Pl. XVI). Plentiful enough for many years, the world demand for commemoratives has almost cleared the market of good copies, and perfect mint examples, always scarce owing to the nature of the gum employed, have been selling at what would have been looked upon as phenomenal prices only a few years ago.

On the other hand there has been a significant lack of demand for hundreds of varieties of early stamps quite attractive in themselves, through the decline of general collecting.

Among these are "middle" issues of the Australian Colonies, Ceylon, etc., particularly where extremely detailed lists are given in the catalogue. Too many kinds of almost identical stamps—identical, that is, except to the expert, and uninteresting except to the enthusiast—have resulted in these stamps receiving only apathetic interest from the majority of collectors. The result has been that nearly all stamps of this type, except those in the most superb condition, are to be seen quoted in advertisements at various fractions of "catalogue". This is often misleading to the uninitiated, who cannot be expected to understand the position. On the other hand, superb examples of stamps of similar design, particularly if they happen to be imperforate, are often unobtainable at even full "catalogue". This, too, mystifies the novice and consequently he looks for something more straightforward. The inexperienced collector, no matter how enthusiastic, cannot reconcile the variations in quotations for what seem to him to be identical stamps. If he is a business man he can easily understand that there must of necessity be differences—but not of such extreme proportions as some of these price variations at first appear.

There has been a remarkable increase, during recent years, in the prices commanded by practically all postage stamps, whether rare or common, or whatever their category, British, Colonial or Foreign; so much so, indeed, that the whole financial position of the collectors' market deserves special and detailed consideration. Let us then examine the economic position of stamp collecting in the light of present conditions, consider its development in the past and attempt to make some estimate of the future tendencies of this most popular of hobbies from the financial aspect. The profit motive, as has been shown, has been predominant in Philately for many years past. World conditions arising largely out of the two world wars have brought about an unusual, and largely unlooked-for, state of affairs that seems likely to continue for some time to come. There are scarcely any stamps that have not advanced in value in the last ten years or so, and what is more, very large numbers have shown substantial appreciation over that period. This has been brought about first of all by the enormous increase in the number of people who collect stamps throughout the world, and secondly for the simple reason that stamps represent an uncontrolled commodity in an almost universally controlled market.

This situation is naturally most satisfactory to the vast majority of philatelists, both amateur and professional, though it does present certain difficulties that may tend to become still greater, so long as prevailing restrictions and circumstances remain. Some of these difficulties arise out of the limitation of imports. In many cases it will be found that the abnormally elevated prices of the commoner kind of stamps are due almost entirely to these controls. Until such time as a free market in stamps is restored the upward trend of prices must be maintained. Meanwhile dealers in the more popular grades of stamps for collections (chiefly required for making into inexpensive "variety" packets) are experiencing much trouble and frustration in obtaining supplies adequate to meet the demands of an ever-growing market.

There are, of course, other and even more potent reasons for the strong upward movement of the stamp market. They are many and varied and some of them have been developing and accumulating over a number of years. Each has tended in its particular way to influence and strengthen the economic background of stamp collecting in all its phases.

For many years, with slight and then very temporary set-backs here and there, stamp values have appreciated, not in Great Britain alone, but all over the world; so that a rare stamp is worth approximately the same in Paris or New York as it is in London or Sydney, thus creating an internationally stabilised market.

Furthermore, between the two wars, really serious inroads were made into the "holdings" of better-class stamps, the investment items, as it were, which were apparent to all who had the opportunity to study the economic side of Philately. In consequence dealers' stocks of the rarer types of stamp were rapidly becoming exhausted, even before the enhanced world demand set in. Because of the ever-growing army of collectors, surpluses formerly held by the stamp trade had been largely absorbed into private collections. Thus really rare specimens and then the less rare but still "scarce" varieties became increasingly difficult to find, when wanted to build up collections. The net result of this excess of demand over supply was to force up prices all round. Popularity, of course, has always played its part in determining the values of stamps. Stamps of "fashionable" countries or groups have at all times commanded higher figures than those less sought after; even when, in point of actual numbers available, they were not so scarce. When the temporary "boom" has subsided the inevitable reaction sets in, but it is seldom that the values of the scarcer items show a really serious decline, once they are absorbed into the regular "catalogue" lists. This principle holds now, as it has done since stamps were first collected, and will continue so long as the quest for stamps by collectors prevails.

In a general way, it may be said that it is demand which controls the value of stamps (except the very commonest, which have practically no cash value as units). On the other hand a stamp must possess some degree of rarity before it can be of any serious worth. A good example of a modern stamp rarity is the 24-cents "air-mail" stamp of the United States in which, through inadvertence, the centre portion was *printed upside-down*. This much coveted "error" (Pl. VI), which was

PLATE VIII

DIE PROOF

←ERRORS
OF COLO[UR]

↓

H. R. Harmer Ltd.

A selection of "Three Cornered Capes" from a famous collection never passed through the post, and of which no more than a hundred examples exist, has on more than one occasion realised over £1,000. The explanation is that "inverted centres" are one of the most popular types of misprint that appeal to philatelists, coupled with the popularity of air stamps in general and those of the United States in particular. By contrast there are several other stamp errors of which fewer copies are known that fetch no more than £50 apiece.

Increase of demand is occasioned by a variety of widely differing causes, some local, others worldwide. Various categories of philatelic material have vogues of varying strength, from time to time. These fashions change, sometimes in an astonishing manner, as may be instanced in the now more popular than ever "Air Stamp" group, which has successfully survived a minor slump only a short time ago, and has staged a brilliant "comeback".

The so-called "classic" issues, represented by the early line-engraved and mainly imperforate stamps issued before 1875, have shown throughout the greatest consistency, but here again discrepancies have occurred, whilst the steady raising of the standard of *condition* demanded by connoisseur collectors has been brought to such a pitch that opinion on the quality of a stamp or piece often varies considerably, even among experts. As the cash value of a specimen depends so much upon the finer points of condition, the less experienced philatelist finds it difficult to arrive at a true estimation where recognised authorities agree to differ. Nevertheless these stamps must be regarded as the "gilt-edged securities" of the stamp market.

CHAPTER V

Philatelic Finance

WITHIN the hundred years or so that the adhesive
postage stamp has been in use the world output of
stamps has steadily grown, slowly at first, but with
ever-increasing impetus; and, contrary to the predictions of
many supposedly shrewd judges, the number of collectors has
risen in at least proportionate volume. At one time the rising
tide of new stamps caused some perturbation among philatelists, both amateur and professional. About midway in the
stamp-collecting epoch, that is to say, some fifty years ago,
and shortly after the dawn of the Edwardian era in Philately,
the collecting of newly issued stamps, particularly those of the
British Empire, came into vogue. To meet this new demand
far-sighted stamp dealers of substance began systematically
to import supplies of all new stamps as soon as they appeared,
passing them on to collectors at a fixed percentage upon "face"
value (and at the same time salting away a proportion for
"stock"). Thus was born the "New-issue service" that is so
strong a feature of stamp collecting to-day.

New stamps had been imported, of course, over a considerable period, but on no scale comparable with that which the
new-issue services assumed at the beginning of the twentieth
century. These made it possible for the collector to obtain
with the minimum of cost and effort a representative showing
of all the latest philatelic novelties, according to his means and
desires. The rich or bold investor could place his order for
singles, blocks of four or even larger items up to the limit of
"face" value, whereas his poorer or less speculative brother
could collect up to the 1s. denomination only. In short everyone could indulge in this attractive method of building up a
collection, with the added incentive offered by the possibility
of obtaining every now and again, and in with the rest, some

short-lived or short-supplied specimen that was destined to appreciate in value almost from the moment of its acquisition. This, in fact, is precisely what did happen, as has been shown at the beginning of the present century, when within a very short time of the appearance of the first stamps of King Edward VII, the pattern of the watermark in paper employed for printing all British Colonial stamps was changed from a single to a Multiple Crown over CA device. As a result of this change values of the earlier printings known as "Single CA's" began to advance, as they were gradually replaced by supplies with the new multiple watermark. This metamorphosis placed an immediate seal upon the new-issues services as an adjunct to modern Philately, thousands of collectors rushing to enroll themselves as subscribers to the services, so as to leave nothing to chance. In their view it became absolutely essential not to miss the elusive variety, and their chief interest was centred upon the arrival of the next batch of new issues, with all that it implied. Further developments in the watermark, design, colour and perforation followed to sustain the collectors' interest, so that the contemporary issues of British Colonial stamps have held the attention of a considerable body of philatelists for the last fifty years or so, and continue to do so.

In the early days some opposition to this novel form of collecting came from dealers and collectors of the old school having large financial commitments in nineteenth-century stamps. They feared that the capital expended on the "new stuff" would leave less to be devoted to the purchase of the older, and in their opinion less speculative, issues. Their fears proved unfounded, however; a slight dislocation may have occurred at the outset, but it was purely ephemeral, and the number of new collectors created by this easy and fascinating form of collecting had, in the long run, a highly beneficial effect on the hobby. The newcomers, in many instances, once bitten with the craze, plunged deeper and deeper into the hobby, eventually extending their interests backwards to the older issues, and so ultimately everyone was happy. The initial opposition was based on the false premise that the amount of money available for investment in stamps was fixed; whereas, as we now know, it is entirely elastic, more so perhaps than most people realise.

It has been shown that the continuance of new issues of stamps in ever-increasing quantities had no injurious effect upon the hobby as a whole. On the contrary the pastime had been strengthened, numerically no less than financially, by extending the scope of philatelic selection.

The so-called "classics" must always occupy the most esteemed position in the philatelic structure, but it is the new issue that performs the missionary work. The stamp-collecting novice is almost always attracted by the novel and the picturesque, particularly when they possess in addition a topical or "news" interest, as they not infrequently do nowadays. His interest thus awakened will extend in due course to other, and earlier, issues, so far as his means and inclination permit.

For a collector, or dealer, to collect or accumulate everything in the way of stamps is practically impossible, even were he to confine himself to the major varieties set forth in the "catalogue". The time factor alone, to say nothing of the monetary outlay, would preclude this. Perhaps some statistically minded person will one day work out the cost of a single stamp collection based upon Stanley Gibbon's catalogue. Even assuming that a large proportion of the material could be bought below catalogue prices, in good condition, numbers of the more elusive stamps would be "out of stock" and some could not be purchased at any price, even over a considerable period. An estimate of a million pounds sterling would probably err on the side of conservatism. A million pounds is a lot of money, but then we do not need reminding that there are a lot of stamps listed by Gibbons. Moreover there are quite a number that few collectors or dealers have seen anywhere, at any time or in any sort of condition. Many of them are little known and not too popular errors or varieties which, though rare, are seldom in demand, but, as the specialist-collector finds to his cost, are not available when they *are* required. This class of stamp, though little known or understood, would alone account for considerable sums in cash.

Then there are the stamps that belong to the "millionaire"

PLATE IX

Frank Godden Ltd.

Stamps of the reigns of King George V and King George VI

PLATE X

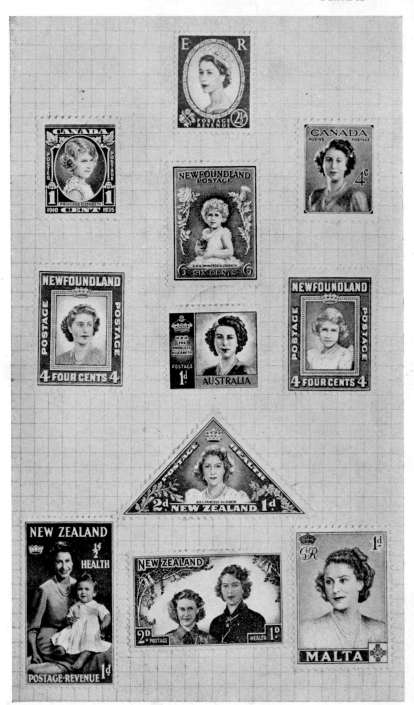

Frank Godden Ltd.

Stamp portraits of Her Majesty Queen Elizabeth II, before
and after her accession

class. The rare early issues made by the United States Post-masters on their own account, the two "Post Office Mauritius" (Pl. XXIV), the unique 1-cent British Guiana of 1856 (Pl. IV) and its modern counterpart the 1-mark Togo "Occupation Franco-Anglaise" of 1915 (Pl. V). The four Hawaiian "Missionaries", in good condition, would cost to-day £10,000 at least. This must be the most valuable of all short sets.

To complete, in perfect state, the early emissions of Canada, Newfoundland, Natal, New Zealand, Ceylon and the Cape of Good Hope, to mention only a few difficult countries, would run into very high figures. Modern stamps, too, would absorb a considerable amount of money, for they have their rarities also, including some highly priced war-time and air-post issues.

Coming down to individual countries, a complete collection of stamps of Great Britain, including Officials, the rare Plate Numbers, Postal Telegraphs and the rest, might cost not less than £25,000. A comprehensive collection of the stamps of many foreign countries, such as France, Switzerland, Mexico, Spain, Brazil and Germany, would be almost as expensive. On the other hand there are lesser states and countries innumerable of which a representative collection might be formed for £100 or so.

It must be remembered that stamps of all nations are collected by somebody and that each and every one has its following of devotees. No matter how uninteresting (philatelically speaking) certain stamps may seem to a particular collector or group of collectors, even in the most sophisticated circles, there is a demand for them, more or less strong, in some part of the stamp-collecting world. Only the essentially international character of the hobby makes possible the varied demand. The biggest dealers who have extensive foreign connections are constantly faced with enquiries for out-of-the-way specimens, which in many instances they are unable to supply at short notice. To keep a stock of stamps anything like approaching completeness is wellnigh impossible nowadays, and so there has sprung up the specialist dealer with a limited field of activity, such as air-mails, modern colonial

4*

issues, or stamps of individual countries such as Great Britain, the United States, etc., who caters primarily for the specialising philatelist.

The strength and stability of Philately varies naturally in different parts of the world, particularly as regards the financial aspect. In the aggregate the most valuable holdings will be found in Great Britain and the United States. Collections of considerable value exist, of course, in Canada, Australia, and South Africa. India, too, was until recently a philatelic market of real importance. South America has many wealthy collectors, whilst some of the largest collections are (or were) in French hands. Switzerland, Sweden, Holland and Belgium are probably the most active centres of Continental Philately to-day.

In addition to the requirements of the general run of buyers who purchase stamps for their collections or for resale to other collectors, the unsettled state of finances all over the world has caused stamps to assume the nature of an investment commodity of world value. Restrictions placed upon Stock Exchange dealings in the early stages of the 1939–45 war led numerous small investors to seek a fresh outlet for surplus capital. Many of them found this in stamps, either as a speculation pure and simple or a long-term investment. In short, stamps, viewed from the financial angle, have shown stability in an unstable world. Small wonder, then, that stamp prices continue to rise with this extra demand of quasi-philatelic investors added to the ever-strengthening requirements of genuine collectors everywhere.

CHAPTER VI

Money in Stamps

STAMP COLLECTING is a world-wide pursuit, and in normal times the philatelic importer and exporter is in the fortunate position of being able to deal with all parts of the world, with a minimum of trouble, through the medium of the post. It is probably true to say that, in spite of controls and restrictions now in operation, seventy-five per cent of all philatelic business is transacted by post. The portability of stamps as a commodity has been a great factor in popularising the hobby.

London has been, for many years, the hub of the world trade in stamps, due to its central position between East and West, which ensures an extensive entrepôt trade. Consequently more stamp dealers and philatelic auctioneers are to be found within a mile or so of Charing Cross than in any other city of the world. The Strand, most famous of all philatelic thoroughfares, has been called "The Street of Stamps". At one time the heart of the philatelic world was in Paris, whilst to-day New York is becoming as important a centre of Philately as it is of Finance. Nassau Street, "down town", is second only to the Strand in the number of its stamp dealers' establishments.

Something like one-third of the world's stamps have been issued in the British Commonwealth and Empire, and this in itself is a dominating factor in making London the keystone of the philatelic structure. The Continent of Europe accounts for an enormous number of stamp collectors, large and small, though not consistently on the same grand scale as in Great Britain and the United States, which together hold the greatest value in philatelic collateral.

The United States now has, and has had for a long time, an enormous number of collectors of stamps of all kinds, from beginners in their hundreds of thousands to the leading specialists. The chief preoccupation of numbers of American collectors, after graduating from the novice stage, is the study of the stamps of their own country. Specialisation of United States stamps has been carried to the extremes of detail, even in modern stamps, and many dealers, as well as collectors, devote their entire time and energy to this phase of Philately.

Philatelists of the United States, however, are not exclusively devotees of their native issues. Stamps of British North America and the West Indies, as well as twentieth-century issues of the British Colonies generally, have a considerable following, whilst some important collections of air-mail stamps are to be found across the Atlantic.

With an estimated figure of two million American collectors to cater for, the stamp trade of the United States is naturally on a large scale. Prices for really first-class material rule high; often higher than British catalogue quotations. On the whole, however, American dealers do not hold such extensive or varied stocks of rare stamps as their London confrères, and for this reason London serves largely as a clearing house for New York, especially where fine stamps of the United States themselves are concerned. Bombay, Johannesburg, Sydney, Auckland, N.Z., Cairo, Paris, Geneva and Buenos Aires all have their individual stamp marts, with dealings principally in the stamps of their own or adjacent countries. Bombay, for example, handles most issues of the Far East, Cairo those of the Middle East, Johannesburg, the African countries south of the Equator, Sydney and Auckland issues of Australasia and the South Pacific. While Paris is concerned chiefly with French and French colonial emissions, supplemented by modern Europeans, Geneva is to-day one of the principal centres for fine old stamps. Buenos Aires, it goes without saying, is the hub of the South American stamps trade. In point of fact the difference in valuations, allowing for fluctuations in rates of exchange, is very slight. Indeed, for the rarer specimens the price is practically the same in any of the philatelic capitals.

By the opening years of the present century stamp collecting was already firmly established and its financial position undeniably strong. As much as £30,000 had been paid for a stamp collection; a single rare stamp, the twopenny "Post Office Mauritius", had realised the then record sum of £1,450 at auction; a leading stamp business, including stock, had been acquired by another firm of dealers for a price said to have been in the neighbourhood of £90,000—and those in the know considered it a bargain at the price. About the same time a specialised collection of British stamps (belonging to the late Earl of Crawford) changed hands for some £16,000, and "deals" of four figures between collector and dealer were commonplace.

Scarce "pieces", i.e. pairs and blocks of certain stamps, plentiful enough as single specimens, were fetching prices out of all proportion to a commensurate rate based on single component copies. The "Penny Black", from being a sixpenny stamp, had jumped to ten times that figure for really fine copies. Round about the year 1904 the hobby may be said to have consolidated its financial position, from whatever angle it was viewed. Stamp collecting was indeed booming as a hobby for the rising generation. Furthermore, professional and business men were collecting stamps, often on widely diverging lines and on scales of varying magnitude. Valuable research work was being undertaken by serious philatelists and societies of stamp collectors were everywhere springing up. Dealers and collectors possessing valuable stocks or collections had by now few misgivings as to the soundness of their holdings. Only the outbreak of a European war, it was considered, could possibly jeopardise the financial integrity of philately.

The European war did break out, as we know, in 1914, but far from stamp collecting being finished, or even severely set back, it actually took on a new lease of life after the first few months. With the advent of the first "war stamps" public interest was revived in no uncertain manner, and the spring of 1915 found the stamp market more active than it had been before the outbreak of hostilities. The same processes have repeated themselves during the World War II as had been anticipated by those who had the experience of the first conflict to look back upon. Although the ramifications of the stamp market had become infinitely greater in between the two wars, the essential principles remained the same and financial reactions tended to follow similar lines.

Towards the end of the World War I it was prophesied that the British market would be flooded with collections and hoards (of unspecified magnitude) from the Continental countries. In particular vast quantities of the more valuable old issues of the German states, accumulated over a period of years, would be let loose, and in consequence the London dealers would be inundated with these hitherto elusive stamps. The threatened avalanche of stamps issued before 1914 failed to materialise and supplies from Europe were never more than a little over normal, Continental dealers and collectors showing remarkable reluctance to part with the better-class material, which they regarded as sound security. Apart from newly created issues and some stocks of ex-German colonial stamps (in unused state), together with supplies of the cheaper stamps and sets, there was little of importance to be bought in Paris, Vienna or Berlin. During the "inflation" period that followed there were bargains to be picked up, but ninety per cent of this material was of the commonest sort, useful only in the "schoolboy" business.

Nor, after the World War II, were any considerable stocks of good stamps unloaded on the London market from abroad. Even allowing for the undoubtedly substantial development of stamp dealing and auctioneering between the wars, it can be taken for granted that stocks of stamps held in this country are, on the whole, lower to-day than they were thirty years ago, even though the number of prospective purchasers is immeasurably greater.

What does this great army of collectors collect? First and foremost, the early imperforate issues from 1840 to 1870, particularly those of the British Empire. These so-called "classics" are the gilt-edged securities of Philately and for this reason are first favourites throughout the stamp-collecting world. Unfortunately a large proportion of collectors are debarred from accumulating these fascinating issues (except in a small way) by the financial outlay involved. There would indeed be many more collectors of "imperforates" if the stamps as a whole were more plentiful or cheaper, hence the growing popularity of the commoner stamps of this period, such as the British "Penny Red".

Fine copies of these stamps are always in strong demand. The time of the quickest increase in the price of imperforate stamps was from 1918 to 1930, when record realisations were made, more especially in the older stamps of Canada, Newfoundland, Australia and most European countries. In the past few years, however, rises in the values of the philatelic "classics" have been less spectacular than those of certain other types of stamps, though good copies have maintained a steady upward tendency.

More recently commemorative stamps of all kinds, both colonial and foreign, have attained a considerable vogue. From the nature of their usage modern pictorial stamps can generally be obtained in lightly postmarked state, so much desired by medium collectors, so that prices usually rule higher for cancelled than for mint specimens. Neither must it be forgotten that the enthusiasm for the more lately issued commemorative has brought the older, and once neglected, picture stamp into new esteem.

Two extremely important phases of Philately, now firmly consolidated in the structure of the hobby, are the collecting of war stamps and the collecting of air stamps. For some time these were treated as separate and distinct branches of collecting, subsidiary to Philately as a whole, but they are now incorporated in the body philatelic. War stamps had been a popular side-line with philatelists from the days of the South African War (1900–02) and may be said to have reached their zenith during and after the world war of 1914–18. Interest in this aspect of Philately received fresh impetus through the special issues associated with World War II. Some of these war stamps are endowed with a high degree of rarity and even the commoner varieties are undervalued by their present catalogue quotations.

The dawn of the flying age, and the increasing use of the aeroplane for the transport of mails, brought into existence a new type of stamp for use on air-borne correspondence. As

a result the collecting of air stamps took definite shape and the
prices of air-mail issues began to increase with the popular
demand. Stamps associated with pioneer flights, such as the
"Hawker" (Pl. VI) stamp of Newfoundland, have risen to
dizzy heights.

War stamps and air stamps do not provide by any means
the only examples of sensational advances in the philatelic
values of stamps issued within the last forty years or so.
Most standard rarities in British Colonial stamps of the present
century have shown enormous increases, more especially for
examples in perfect "mint", i.e. post office state. Stamps of
several Colonies with high face value, always recognised as
scarce, but not always easy to sell on account of their over-
substantial denomination, have come into demand and their
true worth realised. A remarkable instance of this is found in
the £25 stamp of Northern Nigeria (1904) (Pl. V). This stamp
was at one time procurable at round about "double face",
i.e. £50, and never a good seller at that. Suddenly, almost
without warning, its price in the auction room rose to £300
and then to £500. The explanation is that a few collectors of
substance came into the market and, bidding against each
other, discovered that the number of copies available was
negligible.

About the same time the always rare twentieth-century
"Official" stamps of Great Britain came into prominence, in
particular the 10s. and £1 Edwardian stamps overprinted
"I.R.OFFICIAL". The 10s. value (Pl. V) is the rarer, although it
could once be purchased for from £300 to £500. Then one day
the stamp-collecting public woke up to find that, in mint
condition, it was a four-figure stamp. A very small number of
would-be purchasers was sufficient to send up the price at
which it stands to-day (£2,000)—the most valuable though
not quite the rarest single stamp issued by the British
Government. That distinction is reserved for another stamp
of the same series, i.e. the 6d. (Pl. XXIV) value of King Edward
VII, also with the letters and words "I.R.OFFICIAL" added. As it
happened, this was supplied to the Department on the very
day that an Order in Council decreed that special stamps were

no longer to be used on official communications. Only about a dozen copies survived, five of which passed through the post on May 14th, 1904, two days after. Of the stamps in mint condition, a singleton and a pair are in the Royal Collection at Buckingham Palace, whilst a block of four reposes in the collection formed by a former Duke of Leinster and now in the National Museum at Dublin. It is hard, therefore, to account for the fact that when the only mint copy which had come on the market for many years was sold in a London auction room in March, 1952, it realised only £800; at which figure it was snapped up by a far-sighted stamp dealer "for stock".

From an entirely different angle it is perhaps permissible to refer to the "Silver Jubilee" issues made throughout the British Empire on the occasion of the twenty-fifth anniversary of the accession of King George V, and the reasons for the stability of these comparatively common stamps. Attractive in appearance and of historical interest, they form the most outstanding instance of an associated group of stamps, considered neither from the speculative nor investment point of view. Because their face value was low and they were printed in reasonably large numbers they were within the financial reach of the vast majority of collectors. At the time of their appearance they provided an opportunity for a mild flutter, or alternatively an excellent investment. From a modest beginning of £5 a set they rose sharply to £12, then to £20 and eventually to £40. There had, in fact, never been such a run on any set of stamps previously. They have now settled down at round about £30 the set; a nice capital appreciation for the original holders.

It would be instructive to calculate, if it were possible, the actual increment in capital investment in the philatelic world occasioned by the holding of such a group as the "Silver Jubilee" (Pl. XVI) series. The face value alone would be considerable but, as so many have reason to be well aware, no more than a fraction of their present market worth. Reckoned on the very conservative basis of £25 per set, ten thousand more or less complete sets would account for £250,000, whilst dealers' stocks and speculators' holdings would aggregate more than the figure given; so half a million pounds should not be an over-estimate—not bad for one set of commemorative stamps!

The "Silver Jubilees" had a great deal to do, moreover, with the shape of philatelic things to come. They recreated a demand for pictorial and commemorative stamps of all kinds that had long lain dormant. There was in fact a surprising increase in the popularity of all pictorial stamps immediately after the rise of the "Silver Jubilee" issues. Whether the greatly increased turnover enjoyed by many stamp dealers at that time was universal is open to doubt. Some of those specialising in the older stamps did not immediately benefit but all classes of philatelists have since reaped the harvest, in so much as their holdings have become more valuable through the resultant increase in the number of collectors. The once derided commemoratives have played an important part in strengthening the body philatelic. When one recalls the opposition to this class of stamp some sixty years ago, it is all the more remarkable. Still it is doubtful if any of the older generation of philatelists could possibly have foreseen the boom in pictorial commemorative stamps that was so strong a feature of the stamp collectors' market in the nineteen-forties.

The spectacular rise in value of the "Silver Jubilees" was not repeated in the case of the "Coronation" (Pl. XVI) series that ushered in the reign of King George VI. This was due in some part to the smaller face value as well as to the much larger numbers that were sold, i.e. 149,000 as against a mere 23,000 complete sets. The same may be said of the "Victory" issue made throughout the British Colonies in 1946. Conversely, the "Silver Wedding" (Pl. XVI) commemoratives, on account of their high "face", were bought heavily by philatelic investors on a long-term basis, but these have still to mature.

Curiously enough the long chain of special issues connected with the seventy-fifth anniversary of the founding of the Universal Postal Union (sometimes called the "Parliament of Posts"), which appeared throughout the member nations in October, 1949, sprang almost immediately to a premium and is at present one of the best of the associated sets. A possible explanation is that the demand, in this instance, was worldwide and not confined to collectors of British Commonwealth stamps. Generally speaking, however, associated issues with their monotony of design find little favour with either collectors or dealers, principally because of the inroads that they make upon the philatelist's budget and so absorb money that might otherwise be expended on specimens more urgently needed to build up the collection. This fact is coming to be recognised by stamp-issuing authorities, with the result that fewer issues of this category are likely to materialise in the immediate future.

Commemorative issues apart, it should not be forgotten that there are "fashions" in stamps as indeed in most branches of collecting. Just now, so far as English-speaking collectors are concerned, the stamps of individual countries in greatest demand by specialists are those of Canada and British North America generally. (Newfoundland, which formerly headed the list, has fallen to second place since her incorporation in the larger Dominion.) All issues of the British West Indies, both ancient and modern, have a considerable following. After them come the latter-day issues of the Australian Commonwealth, South Africa and New Zealand, with Great Britain some way down the list. Among the lesser Colonies and Protectorates the far-away Falkland Isles, with their Dependencies in the Antarctic, are first favourites. Gambia, with its beautiful "Cameo" issues, on the west, and Kenya on the east are the most popular of British Africans, whilst the colourful stamps of the Seychelles are attracting considerable attention. In Oceania, stamps of the Gilbert and Ellice group are much affected by British philatelists. Malta, after a spell in the doldrums, shows signs of reviving popularity, with Gibraltar a strong second, and Cyprus creeping up for a place.

CHAPTER VII

Postage Stamps and Politics

TO use a stamp to announce some political change is not, in itself, what we mean by "stamp-propaganda": the altering of the centre design on the Naples "Trinacria" so as to replace the lilies of Bourbon by the white cross of Savoy was, in itself, no more "propagandist" than the replacing of Queen Victoria's head by that of her son on the stamps of Great Britain. That it was propaganda in the case of the alteration of the "Trinacrias" is certain, but obviously it is the purpose behind the alteration or the new design which tells us whether or not an issue is to be regarded as propagandist. For instance, when Achmet Zogu was offered the throne of Albania by a (carefully instructed) National Assembly, the change in the stamp-designs of that troubled —and troublesome—country, apart from an improvement in purely artistic quality, was not such as to imply a propagandist intention on the part of the issuing authority. Indeed, the stamps of the Albanian republic which show the bust of Achmet Zogu are far more pretentious than the stamps of the monarchy. There is the change in lettering from "Republika Shqiptare" (Albanian Republic) to "Mbretnia Shqyptare" (Albanian kingdom), but that would be normal even in a country so bound by tradition as is our own. Let us say, then, that the mere announcement of a political change is not *of itself*—though it often is—proof of a propagandist intention on the part of the issuing authority.

And this brings us to the very important aspect of intention; an aspect upon which the whole identification of the propagandist stamp depends.

If we look back into philatelic history, we will be struck by the fact that those who have employed stamps for a propagandist purpose have had their attention called to a stamp's

propagandist qualities by a certain propagandist quality which
has already attached itself to them; in other words, the stamp
has already acquired propagandist qualities before those who
would appreciate those qualities—and would like to use them
—have considered the stamp as a propagandist medium.

This is not difficult to account for. There are always certain
social trends to which the stamp designer, as an ordinary
citizen, is subject. He designs as the citizen of his own country,
and his national prejudices—inherent or acquired—are pre-
disposing factors in his artistic conclusions; no matter what
artists say, they are Frenchmen, or Germans or Italians before
they are French or German or Italian artists; and their
inspiration will inevitably be coloured by the sentiments that
they share with all the other citizens of their own land.

It may well be the fact, then, that it was primarily the
artists who were first responsible for the change by which the
receipt for prepaid postage turned into a medium of propaganda. Indeed, if one examines the stamps of Italy one is
forced to the conclusion that this must be so: that, the artist
having—perhaps unwittingly—shown how a stamp could
convey a nationalistic message, the government accepted their
example, their lesson, and did of malice aforethought what
the artists had done only of their subconscious will.

It is easy enough to see what one knows to be there, but
even if one had not known that Italy, from a collection of
forcibly united petty states, had come to be a great Continental
power, ruling at one time over a large and in many respects
an extremely well-managed colonial empire—all this, be it
noted, within the space of fifty years—a study of the Italian
stamp-issues during that period would have hinted that something important was happening to the country.

Let us take the first issues, which covered the period of the
final unification. The head of the king is crudely designed;
it is a mere syr bol, not a portrait. It is—just a stamp: that
is all that one may say of it. This is the first issue of Victor
Emmanuel II as "King of Italy United", and the date is
1862 (Pl. XIX) two years after the day on which Garibaldi entered Naples and proclaimed Victor Emmanuel as ruler over a

reunited peninsula. Those two years since 1860 had seen some reverses from the men of the Risorgimento; on August 29th, Garibaldi had been captured at Aspromonte, and for a time the fortunes of United Italy looked bleak, as bleak, indeed, as did her stamps.

But help from Napoleon III was on the way; not help altogether gratuitously given, for if the nephew of Napoleon the Great was to force the Austrians to give up Venetia to the Italians, he was to demand, as the price of his assistance, Savoy and Nice. But even this hard bargain was better than none, and the stamps of Victor Emmanuel which were issued in 1863 seem to reflect something of this tempered satisfaction with events; the face of the king has now come to look like that of a human being, and one full of a quiet confidence in his ability to order matters to his own purpose. United Italy was looking to Napoleon III at that moment when the artist roughed out the designs for the new stamps, and just as, under the influence of Thomas Moore and Byron's "Eastern" poems, the artists of the eighteen-thirties used to make even a view of Smithfield Market look like a scene from the *sôk* of Baghdad, so now, with Napoleon III in mind, the artist has made Victor Emmanuel so nearly resemble the Emperor of the French as to seem his twin. This is symbolical magic; and perhaps the artist himself was not astonished when, three years later, after the Prussians had defeated the Austrians on the bloody field of Sadowa, Napoleon forced the Austrians to yield up Venetia to United Italy.

These stamps, rather confident than bold, and still preserving something of the old inhumanness in so much as the face is drawn in full profile, were made to serve until the death of Victor Emmanuel II in 1878, a few months before that Congress of Berlin which was to promise an empire (for the picking up) to the new United Italy.

In the following year the stamps of the new king, Humbert I (Pl. XIX), appeared; and how well they reflect the confidence with which his country now faces a future which is destined to make her, surely, the great Mediterranean power? From a medallion, the head of the monarch has become a portrait; his neck ends now, not in a conventional cutting, but in a military collar, trimmed with gold lace, and his face has turned away from the contemplation of the wall, and now looks, three-quarters full, out of the frame. The lettering, too, has become bolder, the frame less modest; there are curves now, and what one feels is an invitation to celebrate a triumph with the victor And whereas there was no crown on the issues of the first king of United Italy, the new king feels secure in the possession of his artificially contrived, nine-year-old kingdom. One of the designs shows, instead of the king's face, the arms of Savoy, the white-crossed shield encircled with the collar of the Order of the Annunciation. And the crown which surmounts the shield is as bold as may be: there is no mistaking it for a crown. Indeed, it reminds us in shape and in size—but especially in size—of the crown that Napoleon used to employ to mark his imperial dignity. Humbert I is no emperor yet; but one feels, in looking at this stamp, that the designer had hopes of his becoming so.

There were new issues in 1891, and the king, besides looking older—which is what we would have expected—looks sterner; and history tells us why. The French have double-crossed him over Tunis, and the British, in sending an expedition under Sir Garnet Wolseley, have jumped his claim to Egypt.

In 1900 King Humbert was assassinated, and in the following year both Queen Victoria and the Empress Fredric of Germany died, while President McKinley fell by the assassin's hand: it was a period of high mortality among the great ones of the earth.

King Humbert was succeeded on the throne of United Italy by the man who was, save for the brief "reign" of his son, to be Italy's last monarch, Victor Emmanuel III. In spite of the inauspicious circumstances of his accession, he came to power at a time when the foreign policy of the kingdom had been established through the work of a man who died in the year following that in which King Victor Emmanuel succeeded his father: Francesco Crispi, the greatest Italian statesman since Niccolo Macchiavelli. Italy had thrown in her lot with the Prussia who, at Sadowa, had saved United Italy. The young Kaiser was showing himself an active disturber of the peace, and his obvious willingness to blackmail the less aggressive elements of the Continental family promised admirable dividends both for himself and his associates. With such an ally as Germany, Italy had nothing to fear from France.

The confidence of the Italians in their having found themselves on the winning side is well shown by the designs of the first issues of the new reign. The king's head still faces three-quarters, but there is a flamboyance in the decorative frame which surrounds the face which was entirely absent in the designs of the previous reigns (Pl. XIX). And now, for the first time in Italian philatelic history, we encounter that sinister Mascot of the Trouble-makers, the Eagle, which appears on those stamps not showing the king's head. The one-centesimo brown, of 1901, shows, it is true, a small, still very heraldic eagle, with rather more arabesque decoration than bird, and even though on the 2c. brown and the 5c. green the eagle has grown, he is still heraldically "patternish". But he will grow, as we shall see; and his growth will symbolise the progress of those imperialistic plans that he symbolises.

The stamps of 1905 provide the philatelist-philosopher with a curious object-lesson in psychology, and the significance of their designs may be interpreted only by referring to the events which were contemporary with their manufacture. For the three designs are to be taken as the three sections of one conception: the 5c. and 10c. go back in feeling to the later issues of Victor Emmanuel II. They are plain to the point of bareness: the king's head is shown as it would be on a coin of a period; the surround is lacking in the ornateness which characterised the issues of 1901; there is neither crown nor eagle—in short, the stamp tells us nothing by itself.

But taken in conjunction with the other two designs of that 1906 series the plainness of the 5c. and 10c. tells us a great deal. For the 15c. and 20c. show us a very different head: a portrait, this, and one in which the military uniform of the wearer is plain to see. The design is severe enough; only a narrow label at the top of the stamp bears the simple

PLATE XI

Stamps of the Victorian era, 1840–1901

PLATE XII

Stamps of the Edwardian era

legend: "Poste Italiane", and the stamp's value. The rest of
the stamp is devoted to the portrait, which is of a stern-eyed
man, backgrounded by the wide sea, and illuminated by the
rays of a sun which appears to be the ancient Egyptian solar
disc, upheld by the twin asps, until we see that the solar disc
is, in reality, the crown of the New Italy, and that the "asps"
are nothing but the ribands of the crown; though it is impossible to deny that the artist was, consciously or otherwise,
affected by the ancient Egyptian original. Here is symbolism
with a vengeance: the emergence, shy perhaps, but certain,
of that old identification of the king with the sun, with the
principle of life, which in earlier times so strengthened the
power of the crown.

In the third of the three new designs (Pl. XIX), for the values
of 25c., 40c. and 50c., the symbolism is even clearer, and the
three designs are seen, taking it as a pictorial climax, to be
three parts of a whole.

In this third design the king has raised his eyes to the sun,
which is now seen to be identified, not merely with kingship
in general, but with a particular manifestation of kingship:
no less, indeed, that that of His Majesty Victor Emmanuel III,
King of Italy, Cyprus and Jerusalem, Duke of Genoa and
Savoy and Prince of Piedmont. The imperial idea has been
defined in no ambiguous manner; for the "sun" to which
the king is raising up his eyes is the coat of arms of his House.

There is a deep significance in this graphic representation
of the king's awakening, as it were, to the bright promise of
his imperial destiny; but we feel that the artistic concept was
rather dictated by the artist's awareness of unfolding fact.
One feels here that the fact has inspired the propaganda, and
not the other way about; that the artist drew, designed, as the
citizen of a land which was exalted in the knowledge of great
things done, boldly confident in the expectation of greater
things to be accomplished. Here the artist is not working as
the servant of the government, but as a willing collaborator,
perfectly able, of his own inspiration, to provide all that is
necessary for the honouring of the state and the propagating
of its political tenets. And historical record tells us why the

5

artist felt as he did, why he needed no instructing, no prompt-
ing, to draw as he did. Italy, ally of Germany and Austria
since 1882, had drawn ever closer to the Central Powers, and
though France and Russia had formed a "defensive" alliance,
intended to be a counterweight to the Italo-Austro-German
alliance, matters had gone from bad to worse with Russia.
Togo had blown Admiral Rozhdestvensky's fleet to bits, and
had taken Mukden with the loss of seventy thousand Russians,
killed or captured. Port Arthur had gone to the Japanese, and
Russia had signed an ignominious admission of total defeat
at Portsmouth. Then the great empire faced the graver
dangers of internal dissension: St. Petersburg, Moscow and
Odessa exploded into revolt, and the barricades went up in
the streets. Where was France's ally now? How strong was
the anti-Central-Powers alliance now? Italy had all the feelings of the gambler who finds that he has backed the winner.

What was more, that lucky choice was showing results.
France, feeling herself isolated in a hostile Europe—for King
Edward had not yet brought Britain and France into alliance
—embarked upon a policy of "appeasement"; and Italy was
not slow to plead her claims to "justice". The Tripartite
Agreement sought to keep matters as they were without
making them worse; and though France, for all her uneasiness,
declined to give up Tunis to the Italians, she did agree, in
concert with Britain, to divide up Abyssinia, as ancient Gaul
had been divided, into three parts; one for France, one for
Britain and one for Italy. You may see all the awareness of
these encouraging facts in the designs of the 1906 Italian
issues.

But with those issues we take our leave of the undirected
propaganda; we feel that the artist, as a free-lance propagandist, has had his day. For the stamps which were issued in
1911, to mark the Jubilee of United Italy—"symbolic", as
the catalogue tells us, "of the Genius of Italy and the Glory
of Rome"—are stiff with the calculated pretentiousness of
governmental propaganda; they are no more artistically
inspired, no more spiritually spontaneous, than a Bernard
Partridge cartoon in *Punch*. The government has seen the

immense advantages of stamp-propaganda, and except for the brief period of national disillusion after the war of 1914–18 the government dictated the designs, and the artists merely carried them out.

*   *   *

The first three-quarters of the nineteenth century were, for Prussia, as they were for Savoy, years of striving for hegemony over the lesser states by which they were surrounded; and in 1870 both Hohenzollern and Savoy realised their ambition. With the conquest of the Papal States, Italy was at last united; and with the proclamation of the German Empire in the Palace of Versailles, Bismarck's bloody life-work saw its logical fulfilment.

In 1888 two German Emperors died, and "Big Willie" (as we used to call him in the time of the World War I) succeeded to the throne; if there were those who, unlike Queen Victoria, entertained the notion that a peace-loving prince had assumed the imperial diadem of Germany, the first stamp issue of the new Emperor ought speedily to have disillusioned them. True, the first stamps of the German Empire—issued in 1872—had been embossed with what we have called the Mascot of the Trouble-makers, the Eagle (Pl. XVIII), and on the 3 and 5-pfennige issues of 1875 appeared the imperial crown of Charlemagne, but it is impossible to overlook the significance of the change which has come over the eagle in the years between 1872 and 1889.

In the issues of 1872 he is quite a harmless fowl; more heraldically correct than naturally fearsome. His expression is not so much harmless as vacant, and he is crowned, not with the diadem of Charlemagne, but with the cap of maintenance of mediæval German chivalry. By 1875 he has sprouted more feathers, and these seem to bristle in a decidedly aggressive manner (for France, beaten to her knees in 1870, had made a recovery which was astonishing the world and causing Germany to contemplate another war). And since, by 1889, France had grown more powerful than she had been even when Napoleon III was the arbiter of Europe, the rebuke and the warning that Germany feels impelled to give to the beaten who has refused to lie down. Who was responsible for the unambiguousness of the symbolism inspiring the first issues of the new Emperor? The Kaiser himself? The government officials? The artist, self-inspired? It is hard to say; but that is because, in Germany, the views of the mass of the people have almost invariably coincided with the government will. Left to himself, almost any German artist not of a radical attachment would have produced something like the stamp at which the writers invite the reader to take a good look.

The three lower values of the 1889 issue—the 2, 3 and 5-pf. (Pl. XVIII)—carry the crown of Charlemagne much more boldly than do the 3 and 5-pf. of 1875, but it is the design used for the higher values which compels our wondering attention. For on these stamps—the 10 (Pl. XVIII), 20, 25 and 50-pf. the Trouble-makers' Mascot was awakened to a malignantly vigorous life; he is not in the same class with the dull bird of the 1872 issue. See him now! Mark how his feathers have ruffled, how his great wings are outspread! How his breast is pouting and how his tongue darts like that of a serpent from between his cruelly curved beak. His claws, too, have grown; grown and outspread. And the talons on them look most businesslike.

There was a mad scramble for *Lebensraum* in the year that this ferocious eagle is engraved to carry the message of Imperial Germany to the four corners of an earth already grown uneasy at the thought of what Germany intends. That year, though, was a year not mis-spent by the Emperor's ministers. It was arranged that Heligoland, which commanded the Kiel Canal, which commanded the Baltic, should be ceded to Germany by Great Britain. Had it remained in Britain's hands, it would have been useless for Germany even to have set about building up a great naval strength. No wonder the Eagle on the German stamps looked so confoundedly pleased with himself.

In 1899 Great Britain renounced her "rights" in the Samoan group of islands in the Western Pacific, an act of generosity on Britain's part which was interpreted by the Kaiser in the typical German manner, as was well shown by his openly declared sympathy for the Boers. Indeed, a policy of "appeasement" got no better results from Kaiser Wilhelm than, forty years later, it got from Hitler. And the 1900 issue of German stamps well reflect the impression that the Kaiser, with his bellicose speeches and calculated international gaucheries, was endeavouring to make upon a nervous Europe. The fighting Eagle has gone for the moment—we shall see it again! And its place is taken by a female with the face and general physique of a storm-trooper, who wears the imperial crown of Charlemagne, grasps the hilt of a sword in a hand like a leg of mutton, and who has covered her massive form in chain-mail. This unprepossessing female is the personification of "Germania" (Pl. XVIII), and though she becomes a little—but not much—more feminine when the stamps are re-engraved in 1916, she stays as the symbol of German aspirations until the stamps of the Weimar Republic replace those of the First Reich.

She is significant, this Wagnerian termagant. For she symbolises brute force—and that was what she was intended to symbolise. The nations have been warned!

There were four other designs in the same series, one of which, the view of the Berlin General Post Office, does not concern us here. The other three concern us very much, for they repeat and emphasise the message intended to be conveyed by the selection of Germania as the symbol of Teutonic ambitions and Teutonic plans. These three are all extravagantly flamboyant, but it is in the 5-mk. red and black that the message is spoken with most force and least ambiguity.

Standing on the steps of a dais, Wilhelm, dressed in a Ruritanian uniform of Cecil de Mille-ish magnificence, is addressing his assembled ministers. An eagle with outspread pinions perches upon the spike of Wilhelm's helmet; stars and chains and ribands glitter upon his tunic; his mantle sweeps around him to the floor of the audience chamber. There is, indeed, no mistaking this scene for the accidental portrayal of some ordinary function; here is the Emperor addressing

his ministers, and, through the medium of the stamp which
has recorded the occasion, the world. And lest the world be
unwilling to read too much into pictorial symbolism, the
legend under the picture makes the meaning of this design
evident: *Ein Reich, Ein Volk, Ein Gott* (Pl. XVIII). You will
remember that Hitler adopted the same motto for his
own use, though, with characteristic modesty, he replaced
the word "God" by the word "Leader".

*   *   *

We know now, for we have had to learn this truth in a
bitter fashion, that the continuity of the German plan for
world-domination was merely interrupted, and not by any
means broken, when Kaiser Wilhelm left for Doorn, and the
"democrats" of Germany set up the Weimar Republic. The
warning which used to be printed, each day, on the *Daily
Mail* of those times, went unheeded: "They will cheat you
yet, those Junkers . . . " They did. But a study of the stamp
designs of post-1918 Germany makes the fact of this continuity
abundantly clear.

There is, of course, the "butter won't melt in our mouth"
period, when the German rulers were protesting against the
savagery of the Versailles Treaty, and hoping (not, as it turned
out, in vain) that a show of deference to "democratic"
principles would enable them to be spared the penalties
usually extracted from the loser, and to build up their national
resources in preparation for another attempt at a world
conquest.

The first issues, after the recalling of the old Imperial
stamps, are—as one would expect—studiously non-commital.
The stamps issued to commemorate the National Assembly
at Weimar show us an oak-tree, a cut-down oak-stump breaking into shoots, and a nude Atlas-like figure which bears a hod
of bricks (Pl. XVIII), rather than a world. ("A little at a time",
would seem to be the idea behind *this* design!) There has been
a conscious attempt to break with tradition in the matter of
the lay-out and treatment; there is something in the plainness
of the designs which reminds one of the high-class socialist

journals of the time. At all events, there is neither eagle nor crown; though on the air-post stamps of 1919 the lettering is in the traditional German script, though somewhat modified.

In 1921, at a time when the German rulers were making their most vehement protests against the iniquity of the reparations that Germany had been called upon to pay, the stamps show us a Germany busy in the harmless pursuits of peace: shoeing, coalmining, reaping, ploughing (Pl. XVIII); and one can guess that it is hoped that those who see the stamps will believe that the blacksmiths are beating the saw-edged bayonets into the scythes that the reapers are using.

The stamps issued for the Munich Exhibition of 1922 are perfectly innocuous, with their simple coat of arms, and though the "dove" on the air-stamps of the same year bears an unfortunate resemblance to a flying-bomb, one would have needed to be in possession of second-sight to realise that.

Charity stamps of 1922 show a most un-Teutonic angel. Miners reappear on the inflationary issues of 1923, and later in the year Wartburg Castle and Cologne Cathedral remind the world of German culture. Then, following a charity stamp which shows us St. Elizabeth of Hungary helping a beggar, we come across a familiar design, and we notice that, instead of bearing the value of 10, 20, 50 milliards of marks, it is valued at a traditional 3, 5, 10, 20 pfennige, and so forth. It is important to note the smallness of the values, as well as that the Eagle has reappeared; for the two facts are part of the same event.

For the year 1923 had seen the greatest financial swindle of modern times—and, what is more, a swindle perpetrated by a constitutionally established "democratic" government: the "re-constitution" of the German currency.

In that almost hysterical self-confidence which seized the rulers of Germany, when they saw that their swindle had succeeded, and that they were not to be called to account for it, the Eagle reappears. One might think that it was to the advantage of the Reich Government to conceal from the rest of the world the fact that they had been responsible for, and

were thoroughly delighted with the success of, this monu-
mental swindle.

At any rate, the Eagle—the Trouble-makers' Mascot—is
back again; and if we study him, from that reappearance, in
1924, to his final development on 1939 stamps issued in
connection with the Apprentices' Vocational Contest, we shall
see how faithfully his physical and mental growth reflect the
recovery of the nation that he has been selected to symbolise.

For on these normal-sized stamps of 1924 he is in the old
heraldic condition in which he was when we first met him on
the first stamps of the German Empire in 1872; he is not life-
like, only decorative, and not very aggressive. His wings point
vertically downwards, and though he is not quite as inoffensive
as he was on the stamps of 1872 he seems harmless enough.

But in the next year of financial liberation he reappears;
and already a significant change has come over him (as,
indeed, it has come over the German nation as a whole). Two
designs, issued ostensibly to commemorate the thousandth
anniversary of the Rhineland confederation, show, on the
second stamp, the German Eagle over the twisting, castled
river (Pl. XVIII). Even the dullest wit could not mistake the
significance of this eagle; grimly predatory, he rises gigantic
above and *behind* the great river which is Germany's natural
frontier. And perhaps we will not be wrong in attributing
his new grimness to the fact that Britain and France were at
loggerheads, that the Dawes Plan had been accepted, and
that the French had agreed, even though reluctantly, to the
evacuation of the Rhineland, which had gravely threatened
the unity of the Reich. United Germany is a conquering
Germany.

For the Rhineland commemoratives the designer had used
only the eagle's head, and to remedy this parcelling up of so
famous a bird, the Munich stamps of a later date in that same
year bear the eagle's wings; and here again one may see the
effect upon the German mentality of Allied squabbling and
Allied simplicity. The wings, which on the 1924 issues pointed
to the ground, are now raised at an angle of forty-five degrees,
and the two thunderbolts which are to come to be associated

with the Hitler Jugend make their appearance for the first
time on a Reich stamp. (Bear in mind, please, that *Mein
Kampf* had already been written by 1925.)

The air-stamps of 1925 unite the eagle into one whole again;
and a vigorous bird he has become. What is more, he has
ceased to be heraldically conventional, and has become life-
like. Pinions raised for the take-off, he scents his prey, and
when again we meet him, on the air-stamps of 1934, he has
reached—once again—his full growth, though this time he is
something bigger than ever he was under the Kaisers. He is
flying now, his vast wings outspread so as to cover half the
world over which he glides, and the sun whose light gilds his
feathers is charged with a swastika; it *is* the swastika, just as,
in the symbolism of the Italian stamps of 1906, the crown
of Italy and the coat of arms of Savoy were the sun itself.

*   *   *

With that picture of the German Eagle on the wing the
stamps of the Second Reich come to an end, and what came
between that date and the final ignominious collapse of
Nazidom in the cellars of the Berlin Chancellery belongs
rather to the department of conscious propaganda: the designs
of the German stamps from 1934 onwards are too obviously
inspired by a formal governmental instruction to betray anything; they do not betray a fact, they simply state it. Up to
the birth of the Fascist state, the artists had worked with the
government, but as individuals rather than as cogs in a governmental machine; their designs reveal to us what the Germans
themselves thought of their condition and expectations. But,
with the conscious employment of propaganda, one may see
only what Hitler and his associates had in mind; the influence
of the people on philatelic design has ceased.

But there is one point which is of great interest: neither
aspect of this (after all, extremely childish) propaganda is
permitted to be neglected at the expense of the other, for all
that it is obvious that half of the total has failed in doing what,
apparently, it was intended to do. Thus, though the Nazi
claim to the restoration of German colonies was gently if

disingenuously brought forward with the issue, in 1934, of a set of portraits commemorating the German Colonisers' Jubilee, and the threatening aspect of this "scientific" propaganda grew progressively less ambiguous until, in the year before the war, it culminated in the incredibly sinister (and extremely well drawn) picture of Hitler in Braunau, the "nicer" side of German propaganda was not denied its fair share of the stamp-issues; so that, among the Brownshirts and swastikas and helmeted warriors of the Air Defence League, we find castles and early steam-engines and peasant girls and a charming maternal scene symbolic (so we are told) of "local" government. And in the very year of the war, when the German boa-constrictor was digesting the first mouthfuls of conquest, a stamp appears in celebration of the seventieth anniversary of the German Derby, and another, bearing an excellent reproduction of a Dürer portrait of a young woman, to celebrate the "Day of German Art", and to bring funds into Hitler's "Culture Fund".

One feels, then, that propaganda may be the wrong word to use in connection with the messages conveyed—or intended to be conveyed—by the stamps of a national government alive to the utility of the postage stamp as a medium of information. For propaganda connotes a certain subtlety; and this announcement of aims and intentions is anything but subtle. Taken as a means of convincing the rest of the world of the justice of one's claims to this and that, the stamp strikes the writers as being of small use; though it may well be valuable as a means of threatening by a hint.

All the same, one feels that the message of the stamp is primarily intended for the people of the issuing country; that it is to *their* emotions that the stamps' messages are principally intended to appeal. It must be so, for this "scientific" propaganda, wherein guns and roses are held to have an equal part, cancels itself out. If Hitler had consistently ordered his philatelic artists to draw only pictures of such castles as Allenstein or Forchtenstein, or pictures of fishing-smacks or early Daimler and Benz motor-cars, well and good; some might have found the justification in those designs for that wishful thinking whereby they had persuaded themselves that Hitler was a man of peace. Or if he had as consistently ordered his artists to concentrate upon such grim warnings as that provided by the picture of the Nazi outside the Munich Feldherrnhalle, the world might—perhaps—have been too terrified to offer any opposition to his plans. But the steel-helmeted warrior of the 1935 "War Heroes Day" issue is cancelled out, as it were, by the pretty postcard scene of Breslau Cathedral. And it was the same with the stamps of Russia and Italy. Indeed, it begins to be certain that there is something in the very nature of propaganda which defeats its own object, and that the more skill is brought to its employment, the less successful will be the results of the propagandist's efforts; that is to say, so far as converting the people of other countries is concerned.

*   *   *

The writers feel that, in the future, stamps will not be produced for the persuasion of the foreigner, but only for the reassurance of the citizen of the country which issues them, and this tendency is already strongly marked in Russia, which now employs its stamps rather as a sort of national pictorial bulletin, bringing to the notice of the Soviet citizen the national achievements in art, science and architecture; recalling to the citizen great historical traditions, and the names and faces of those associated with the most glorious epochs of national life. The orders of chivalry instituted by Generalissimo Stalin are portrayed (Pl. XXII), together with those princes of old Russia—Suvarov, Kutusov and Alexander Nevsky—after whom the orders were named. The policy of the rulers of modern Russia has been, for some time past, designed to restore that continuity of tradition which was broken at the Revolution; to unite the old and the new Russia in the consciousness of the average citizen. Thus, alongside of writers and poets who were despised in the friendly revolutionary nineteen-twenties as "bourgeois", the stamps of Russia carry not only scenes from the time of the establishment of the Bolshevik régime, but a series pointing out the horrors of war, this series obviously designed to uphold the claim that Russia never fights unless provoked.

It is too early yet to say that the stamp designed to carry a message to other countries is finished, but it is more than probable that the stamp's propagandist quality will be directed, in the future, rather to the convincing of the already converted —the home market—than to the persuading of the foreigner.

For there is this in a stamp which is too apt to be overlooked in this consideration of its other qualities: it is an official document, and as such bears that indefinable but authentic air of the governmentally authorised which gives its message the weight of ministerial utterance. The foreigner may attach no great weight to the stamp-messages of other lands, but he will be inevitably swayed by those of his own country's issues; and it will be to him, and not to his foreign cousin, that the messages of the future issues will be addressed.

The writers foresee the stamp used not as a medium of propaganda so much as a medium of governmental advertising; the difference being that propaganda implies a certain deceptiveness, where mere advertising need not palter with the truth.

This tendency is well exemplified in recent stamps of Russia, Chile and the Argentine, all of which make a claim to territory, but rather as registering a fact than as putting forward a claim, however juridically feasible and universally accepted: a claim which (at least in the opinion of the government making it) is of a pre-emptory nature—that is to say, inconvenient to take up immediately, but enforceable, under the common law of international relations, as and when that government wishes to do so.

Nor is this claim-by-postage-stamp a new thing; our first example dates from 1896, a date which roughly coincides with the beginning of American imperialism, as planned by the highly aggressive President Grover Cleveland. It must be remembered that the United States, at the very end of the nineteenth century, found herself in possession of overseas possessions for the first time in her history: Cuba, Puerto Rico, the Philippine Islands and Hawaii. Paradoxically, as it seems, this breaking with her traditional reluctance to own territory outside the American continental land-mass did not mean a falling away from the Monroe doctrine which had been the "justification" for the United States not moving out of America, and her not letting any newcomers in; it simply meant that the Monroe Doctrine received a new interpretation, and that it was in future to be known as Pan-Americanism.

There is no space (nor real need) here to discuss the merits, or otherwise, of the change which came over U.S. foreign policy after the close of the Civil War, but the fact is that the year 1900 saw a United States grown decidedly imperialistic, not only for herself, but in the interests of her "fellow American states".

Perhaps the most significant aspect of the stamp to which we are calling the reader's attention—the Venezuela "map issue" of 1896 (Pl. XVII)—is that it was issued, with the connivance of the U.S. government, two years before the Spanish-American War of 1898, and two years before the annexation of Hawaii by the U.S. government.

One would say, then, that an attempt had been made to find the solution to international problems first by peaceful means, before the harsher measures were relied upon. Alas for that consoling thought! The threat of war accompanied the subtler reasoning of the stamp.

What was this stamp? Officially issued to commemorate the Venezuelan national hero General Miranda, the design showed, as a part of Venezuelan territory, certain adjacent districts of British Guiana, a small matter of some *sixty thousand* square miles!

British Guiana, considered as a Crown Colony, originated in our acquiring it from the Dutch after the close of the Napoleonic Wars. In 1840 a boundary commission, sitting under an independent chairman, confirmed the existing boundaries marking off Venezuelan territory from that of British Guiana, and for many years Great Britain enjoyed the most friendly (and somewhat paternal) relations with Venezuela, after it had freed itself from Spanish domination. In most of the chief towns of the ex-Spanish colonies British postal agencies had been established, and not until the development of the Venezuelan mineral resources by American financial interests did the old happy relationship between Venezuela and Great Britain begin to deteriorate. We have all heard of "dollar diplomacy"; and President Cleveland was an unashamed and vigorous advocate of that sort of diplomacy. With the President's support, the American financiers, disguised as the Venezuelan Foreign Office, laid claim to sixty thousand square miles of British Guiana territory; and so that Whitehall should be under no misapprehension concerning President Cleveland's interest in, and support of, the claim, he wrote a letter to Queen Victoria's government stating that he was, if necessary, prepared to support Venezuela's claim by force.

There was no war: instead, Lord Salisbury suggested to the United States that an International Arbitration Committee be set up under a French chairman, and this was done—a fact which may cause the cynics to smile, seeing that Venezuela was represented by an ex-president of the United States, Benjamin Harrison!

Now it was while the matter of the setting up of the Commission was being considered—was *sub judice*, in the legal phrase—that the "Miranda" stamps appeared. That this was what, in ordinary domestic law, is called gross contempt of court was apparent; and Great Britain, though she signed the Treaty of Arbitration on February 2nd, 1897, made the strongest possible protests against this bit of truly Hitlerian practice. And, with the support of General Harrison, the Venezuelan government withdrew the issue *officially*, keeping to the letter of, and brazenly breaking the spirit of, their undertaking by flooding the philatelic market with "remainders", an action which clearly demonstrates the true purpose of the stamp ostensibly issued to commemorate General Miranda.

Nor is it without interest to recall that the decision of the Committee, in October 1899, gave Venezuela, not sixty thousand, but *two hundred* square miles, and that, in return, Great Britain was given the free navigation of the Barima

and Amakeru rivers. More, the great Venezuelan revolution
of 1899–1900 was a direct result of the arbitration award: so
that the stamp as a propagandist medium may be said, in this
instance, to have had results certainly not envisaged by its
issuers.

But perhaps not every king or president is a philatelist, as
were the late King George and President Roosevelt; for, in
1936, the Argentine government decided to use this somewhat dubious weapon of the stamp-made claim to affirm its
"right" to the British-owned Falkland Islands (known to
them as the "Islas Malvinas").

The stamps of this issue show South America, with the
various states outlined but not marked in any way. Only the
Argentine and the Falkland Islands are shaded (Pl. XVII): the
assumption being that we are intended to accept the shading
as a "proof" of the indivisibility of the Islands from their
parent Argentine. That on the smaller values of a contemporary issue is portrayed the head of a prize shorthorn bull
belonging to an English rancher in no way detracts from the
impudence of the Argentine claim to territory which has been
owned and administered by Britain for over a century, though
it is only fair to add that the Argentine issue was in all
probability provoked by the British centenary issue of 1933.
They even went to the petty length of treating as "unpaid"
any letters arriving in the Republic under frank of the
"offending" Falkland Islands stamps!

But for the latest example of Argentine philatelic propaganda no such excuse may be found: a piece of propaganda,
of the "claim" type, which also involves territory hitherto
considered indisputably British.

The new Argentine stamp, whose legend reads (translated)
"First Antarctic Post—Argentine Republic—22 February
1904–1947", was issued, so we are informed, to commemorate
first the establishment of an Antarctic postal service in 1904,
and, second, the engagement of the Argentine government's
ships in the Polar exploration that so many nations—including
our own—are at present undertaking. The design of the stamp
shows the "Argentine Antarctic Sector" clearly marked, and

the sector is tinted to indicate the Argentine "right" to it. The fact that the "sector" includes the Falkland Islands, South Georgia and the South Shetlands clearly indicates that Argentine appetites have grown considerably since the 1936 issue of the now relatively modest claim to the Falklands alone.

But an interesting—indeed, amusing—situation has arisen between the Argentine and her neighbour republic, Chile. For Chile, too, has joined in the craze for Polar exploration, and she, too, issued a stamp, not only to commemorate the fact, but to put on record, for all the world to see and to ponder over, that "by the Decree No. 1747 of 6.XI. 1940", she made formal claim to the territory claimed by the Argentine on *her* stamp! But if the stamps do nothing more, their appearance does at least prove that the fashion for making statements of an international significance through the medium of a country's stamps must flourish more fully before it dies away altogether: for it has obviously taken a firm grip upon the fancy of those with international (and impudent) demands to make.

Britain's rejoinder was to place a map of *her* Antarctic territorial claims upon some definitive stamps provided, in 1946, ostensibly for postal use, but more particularly for political prestige, by the scattered post offices of the Falkland Islands Dependencies from South Georgia to Graham Land (Pl. XVII). Thus a "cold war" continues to be waged in the South Polar regions by means of opposing issues of stamps.

At the other end of the world something not dissimilar is happening: for the United States, through her possessions and alliances and—as she prefers to call them—her "neighbours", spans the globe from the Arctic to the Antarctic Circles, and the North Pole figures on "claim" issues of stamps just as does the South Pole. You will recall that, in 1931, the German airship *Graf Zeppelin* made a world flight which aroused considerable public interest, and which was commemorated on the stamps of many of the nations over which the giant dirigible passed. The Russians gave the airship what is sometimes called a "good press" and one design was issued in connection with the *Graf Zeppelin's* Polar flight.

Now note that, in the following year (1932), Russia issued

PLATE XIII

ANIMAL STAMPS

Tapir; Tiger; Asiatic Elephant; Kangaroo; Puff Adder; Emu; Orang-
outang; Wild Deer; Rhinoceros; Roussa Stag; Caribou; Argus Pheasant;
Tropical Fish

PLATE XIV

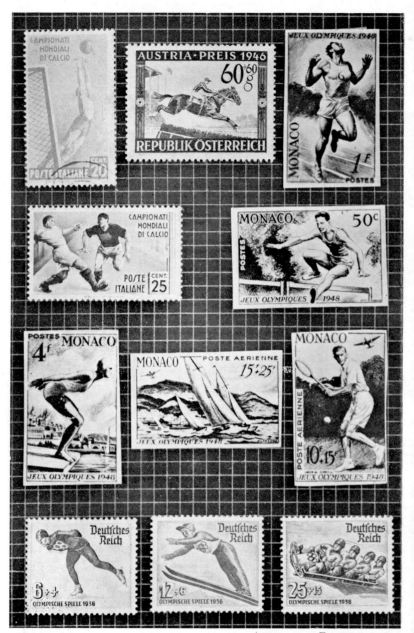

SPORTS ON STAMPS

Football, Horse-racing, Running, Hurdling, Diving, Yacht-racing,
Lawn Tennis, Winter Sports

an air-mail stamp, ostensibly to commemorate the flight from Franz-Josef Land to Archangel and the work of the Soviet ice-breaker *Sibiriakov*, but in reality to establish the precedent of showing the North Polar regions on a Russian stamp. This tentative approach to what was later a formal claim to Polar sovereignty bears the legend, "International Polar Year—1932–3"; and its precedentary quality is amply proved by the issue, five years later, of stamps commemorative of the first trans-Polar flight—a flight whose significance takes on deeper meanings when we observe that it was carefully timed to coincide with the twentieth anniversary of the foundation of the Red Army. There were two separate issues commemorative of this flight, one commemorating the flight proper, the other those aviators who made the historic air voyage, but both sets showed the Soviet flag firmly planted on the North Pole.

In yet another attempt to "twist the Lion's tail" stamps have been used to bolster up an ingenious claim put forward by the Central American republic of Guatemala to the whole of the territory which for more than a hundred years has constituted the Crown Colony of British Honduras. The claim has been rejected by H.M. Government, with an offer to refer the dispute to the International Court of Justice at The Hague, but meanwhile a miniature map shown on the 5-centavos Guatemalan stamp embraces the whole of British Honduras as part of Guatemala. To this H.M. Government replied with a set of stamps commemorating the 150th anniversary of the Battle of St. George's Bay, when a Spanish attempt to invade British Honduras was effectively repulsed by the Royal Navy.

A more recent and flagrant invocation of the power of the postage stamp for political propaganda lies in the overprinting of contemporary Egyptian stamps with the titles then newly assumed by ex-King Farouk, i.e. "King of Egypt and the Sudan". Followed a set of pictorial stamps, similarly inscribed, in an attempt to bolster up Egypt's one-sided abrogation of the Anglo-Egyptian Treaty of 1936, and further to anticipate a repudiation of the treaty made between the two nations as far back as 1899 in relation to a joint administration of the Sudan.

6*

CHAPTER VIII

Propaganda by Postage Stamp

PROPAGANDA—a word which has become excessively familiar to the reader of the newspapers since the collapse of the old Europe in the social disturbances following the war of 1914–18—is yet another of those words which have acquired a progressively worse meaning as they have grown older: for the first recorded use of *propaganda* (Latin for "that which is propagated") in a specialised sense is in the title of the Society for Propagating the Faith, which was founded at Rome in 1622. It has now acquired the meaning of a propagation of views by possibly dishonest and always disingenuous ways. As all of us have become too nauseatingly familiar, not only with the modern use of the phrase, but as well with the practice that it describes, there is no need to explain further here the nature of "propaganda".

Great Britain, as regards its governmental tradition, has most conscientiously striven to remove certain state activities from the modifying effects of human prejudices: the stamps of this country, while—on the whole—dull, as compared with those of many other nations, have been remarkable for an impersonal functionalism. They are stamps: government-authorised receipts for the pre-payment of postage, and not the advertisements of national conceit, of political aspirations. It is inevitable, therefore, that there should have been lapses from the high standard set by those responsible for the framing and carrying out of the provisions of the first Penny Postage Act (1 & 2 Vic., cap. 52) of August 17th, 1839: as when the egregious Postmaster Connell put his own face upon the stamps of New Brunswick, and Colonel (afterwards General) Baden-Powell offended the royal dignity by putting his likeness upon the crude issues of beleaguered Mafeking. But these falls from grace were instantly rebuked and as quickly corrected, and, as far as the home country is concerned, only the strange aberration which envisaged the printing of "Pears' Soap" on the back of penny stamps of 1881 (which, by the way, were never put in circulation), and the issue of the British Empire Exhibition of 1924–25, (Pl. XV) may be called "propagandist" in any sense of the word—in the first case, because the purchaser of a stamp did not expect to be exhorted to buy a popular brand of soap, and, in the second, because the Lion which occupies half the design seems to be telling the world something more than that there is an exhibition at Wembley.

But these few lapses from the rule only go to emphasise how rigidly the rule had been kept: the British government, since 1840, has set its face—and often in spite of much local clamour for commemorative issues—against using its postage stamps as vehicles of propaganda. Alone, of all countries in the world, it has refrained even from marking them with the country of origin, only in one instance—that of the issue commemorating the Postal Union Congress of 1929 (Pl. XV)—putting the word *London* into the legend.

It is certain that it was from a worthy desire to avoid the giving of bad example that our successive governments have set their face against making our postage stamps into posters, and not, as some people contemptuously affirm, from that "stuffy" traditionalism supposed to be inherent in the British nature. Nor, despite the fact that few other nations have refrained from using their own stamps as media of propaganda, has the example been entirely without effect. If other nations do more and more use their stamps to point a national moral or adorn a national tale, there has not, as yet, begun that unrestricted battle of the propagandists which has so often seemed to be imminent, but which has not yet come about. National propaganda has, so far, kept to the more subtle forms of expressions—to the boasting of great national undertakings, mostly, or to the commemorating of great national events— and but rarely have too crudely offended the sensibilities of other nations. And this, of course, is due to the fact that there are still some nations which set a high standard in what we may call philatelic censorship: and if these nations are careful not to offend the susceptibilities of others, they are equally disinclined not to be offended. While such philatelic censorship still obtains, other nations, less careful, must restrain themselves from giving too much offence, or risk the banning of their stamps altogether.

On the other hand, it must be admitted that those governments who cannot resist the opportunity to use that excellent medium of propaganda which every stamp most certainly is have gone as far as they have dared: and to many it will seem that propaganda is not the less offensive because it is subtle. But the moral effect of such restraint as is shown by such governments as those of Britain, Sweden, Switzerland, Iceland and pre-revolutionary Spain (with one sad lapse in the "La Maja" design of the 1930 Goya commemorative—which was hardly propagandist—and one in the stamps of the 1930 Spanish-American Exhibition which most certainly was) has tended to modify the force of stamp-propaganda, keeping it far above the immoderate level to which wireless propaganda descended in the free-for-all period of unrestricted warfare. With stamps, one has merely to refuse to accept the mail from the propagandists' countries. That this drastic method is one which would be employed only after a deal of thought and more of provocation goes without saying, but the U.S. government did consider this serious dislocation of traditional international exchange in 1930, following upon complaints, made by many of its citizens, that letters from Spain were bearing stamps whose design was of an "obscene" nature (Pl. XXI). It was useless for the highbrows to protest that the design in question was a reproduction, on a small scale, of a work of the great Spanish painter Goya: questions were raised in the House of Representatives, and the attention of the U.S. Postmaster-General was called by scandalised Congressmen to the existence of the convenient Comstock Law, which prohibits the entrusting of scandalous matter to the U.S. Mail—makes it, indeed, a penal offence. But even where governments are stirred out of their traditional distaste to take hasty action, the breaking-off of the normal methods by which contact with other states is maintained is an act which merits the longest meditation, the deepest consideration. And by the time that the government has decided to go beyond a mere protest, the act which inspired the protest has become "ancient history"—better forgotten.

*   *   *

To some theologians, all lies are lies—equally bad: the untruth is not to be considered except independently of its inspiration or its effect.

Let us see, in considering the development of propaganda in stamp design, if this important distinction between good and bad propaganda may be upheld.

In the first place, at what period did stamps begin to forsake their original purely fiscal purpose (which in Britain has never been lost and seldom modified) and become the universally disseminated announcements of national pride, ambition, intention or—yes—folly?

The answer is: a good many years before both Mussolini and Hitler were born, and—alas for human nature—not many years after the first postage stamp was issued.

If you turn back to almost the beginning of our period— to 1860, to be precise—you will find an excellent example of what we may call the "propaganda of the *fait accompli*".

Naples was a port of the Bourbon kingdom of the Two Sicilies until the "liberators" of Garibaldi and Cavour forcibly incorporated it into the Savoyard kingdom of United Italy, and in 1858 King Ferdinand II issued that series of stamps which, because their design incorporates the arms of Sicily, Naples and the House of Bourbon, have come to be known among philatelists as the "Naples *Trinacria*" (Pl. XIX). There were eight values—ranging from the half-tornese to the fifty-grano—in the issue, and all were suppressed as soon as the soldiers of the King of Sardinia had caused the Bourbon monarch to fly. But before the stamps of the usurped kingdom of Naples could be replaced by an entirely new issue, the centre of the plate was re-engraved with the white cross of Savoy—which is why these stamps are known among philatelists as "Savoy Crosses".

It is immaterial that the need to spare the public the inconvenience of going without stamps caused the provisional government to utilise, as far as possible, the already existing plate from which the stamps of the dethroned ruler had originally been printed: what concerns us here is the fact that a political change of fundamental importance was recorded, in symbolic form, upon a postage stamp. The world was to see many more events—and some of far more importance—recorded in a similar manner.

*   *   *

Since we have agreed to differentiate between the various kinds of such propaganda as we may meet in the designs of postage stamps, it will be as well here, before we proceed further, to see what these different kinds are.

Let us make an attempt to classify the different sorts of propaganda that stamps, in the hands of other governments than our own, are intended to disseminate.

First of all, let us consider general propaganda. This is always designed to prove to the world two things: one, that a country is more civilised than general opinion usually credits her with being; the other is designed to prepare the world for a favourable reception of acts which are contemplated by the governments of the issuing countries. In the first instance only countries under an international cloud—what many will call backward countries—go in for this form of national self-praise, which is really the expression of national touchiness, if not of national guilt-consciousness. In the second instance, it is rarely that small nations are to be found indulging in this sort of propaganda: for small nations are forced, by their smallness, to be content to survive, and may not look forward to conquest. The greatest exponents of the second sort of general propaganda have been Italy and Germany, but they have a chapter to themselves. When, though—to anticipate—we bear in mind that Russia, Haiti, Mexico, and the Dominican Republic have been great exponents of the first (self-praising, self-justificatory) sort, and, as we have seen, Germany and Italy of the latter ("selling the idea") sort, we can begin to appreciate the difference between the two types of general propaganda, and also to note the close connection between the national sentiment and the design of the national postage stamps.

With regard to the particular type of propaganda, this may be divided up still more, for quite often a general sentiment will cause a government to take particular advantage of it to issue perhaps one stamp: the expression of a lasting national prejudice, but designed only to annoy one particular state at one particular time. Let us take an example, to make matters clearer.

When, in 1922, the newly constituted Irish Free State issued the first stamps specially designed to its order, one of the four marvellously restrained designs (in a political sense, of course) bore a map of Ireland: a map which quite ignored the implications of the treaty which had just been signed, since it showed the Green Isle as one political unit. The purpose of the design is obvious: as it is obvious in that of another stamp of the same series, which shows a shield, quartered with the arms of the four provinces, including Ulster. But the oft-reiterated claim of Mr. de Valera to Northern Ireland has not, since that first issue of stamps, formed the inspiration of Eire's stamp designs, Mr. de Valera's government having, in its later issues, rather striven to emphasise the religious and cultural aspects of the republic.

And even though, by inference, that stamp of 1941, which was issued to commemorate the twenty-fifth anniversary of the Easter Rebellion of 1916 (Pl. XXI), may well be accepted—and was, in Ireland, so accepted—as of an anti-British character, the Sinn Fein sentiment is remarkably subdued, and anyone who wishes to see in it merely the normal commemoration of an important historic event is quite justified in doing so.

We may, then, say that stamps to be classified as under the heading "particular propaganda" are to be divided up as follows:

(a) Issues commemorating a national event, achievement, personage or characteristic, with no intention other than to gratify national self-esteem.

(*b*) Issues commemorating the same things, but with the purpose, more or less explicit, of persuading other nations that the value of the nation issuing the stamps is different from the opinion generally held.

(*c*) Issues intended to advertise the country of origin, either for the simple commercial purpose of attracting visitors, or to persuade other countries to accept a *fait accompli*.

(*d*) Issues intended to annoy another or some other countries.

(*e*) Issues intended to express "solidarity" with some international movement.

(*f*) Issues intended to do for the person of the ruler what has been done, for the nation, by *a*, *b*, *c*, *d*, and *e* above.

(*g*) Issues intended to proclaim a national "right" to something or other.

Of all these classes, only *a* and *e* can provide us with examples of "good" propaganda, and even with these there is almost always bound to be so much national prejudice associated with laudable national pride that *someone—somewhere*—is sure to be offended. For most national events, save those which commemorate the opening of some canal or museum, seem to be associated with the breaking-away of one state from another; certainly a great many celebrated personages represented on the stamps of recent years have been eminent divines, scientists and literary men, but there have also been a large number of revolutionaries, who are not likely to be popular with the states against which they rebelled. As for class *e*, here again we may meet with as much "bad" propaganda as "good", since, though stamps commemorating, say, the International Eucharistic Congress, the Olympic Games, the flight of the airship *Graf Zeppelin*, the International Red Cross, Esperanto or Children's Day may not be regarded, *per se*, as other than admirable, it is astonishing to what base uses human perversity may turn even laudable internationalisms of this sort. No one will find any fault with

PLATE XV

Frank Godden Ltd.

BRITISH COMMEMORATION STAMPS

Wembley Exhibition, 1924; U.P.U. Congress, London, 1929; Silver
Jubilee, 1935; Coronation, 1937; Postage Stamp Centenary, 1940;
"Peace", 1946; Olympic Games in London, 1948; Seventy-fifth anniver-
sary of founding U.P.U., 1949; Festival of Britain, 1950

PLATE XVI

COMMONWEALTH "COMMEMORATIVES"

Diamond Jubilee, 1897; Silver Jubilee, 1935; Coronation, 1937; "Victory and Peace", 1946; Silver Wedding, 1948; Seventy-fifth anniversary of Universal Postal Union, 1949

the Soviet authorities for having, on their Zeppelin commemorative design, shown the huge airship above the wonderful
Dnieperstroi Dam: the artist had to put the Zeppelin over
something, then why not (killing two birds with one stone)
praise German and Russian achievement on one stamp? But
the uniting of the heads of Pope Pius XI and King Alfonso XIII
on a Spanish stamp of 1928, issued to aid the Catacombs
Excavation Fund, was eagerly seized upon by the enemies
both of the Spanish monarchy and Catholicism generally as
the "proof" of heaven-knows-what conspiracy to replace a
Bourbon on the throne of the Two Sicilies, or to bring Spanish
South America under the Spanish crown, or a dozen other
things, all as equally absurd and all as thoroughly believed.
For propaganda has a nasty habit of "coming back" at the
propagandist, which is one of the best arguments in favour
of Great Britain having handled propaganda generally with
extreme reluctance, and so far as her stamps are concerned—
not at all.

*   *   *

Indeed, when we consider the propaganda motif of most of
to-day's stamp issues—and as time passes, most stamps become
increasingly propagandist in essence—we are struck by the
fact that very little indeed of all this propaganda is innocent,
though it may be, and often is, perfectly harmless. Man is a
rationalising animal, and he is never more completely at his
happiest than when he is rationalising into righteousness what
he feels awkwardly to be a fault. And it is, indeed, too fatally
easy for a government to find excellent reasons why its stamps
should bear, to the farthest corners of the world, some message.
We live in an age whose greatest boast is its "practicality",
and one may imagine the practical men who are in charge of
nations' destinies looking upon the non-message-bearing
stamp as an affront to all that is practical (and therefore, by
modern ethical values, perfect). Let us not forget that the
stamp—even the propagandist stamp—is much older than
wireless-telephony, and not so long ago was the only means
whereby the subtle form of propaganda of which it may be

7

made the medium was able to penetrate into the countries both
of friends and of enemies. For newspapers, by their very
nature, may not be subtle propagandists: a newspaper which
seeks to convert subtly is unintelligible.

Back, then, to the consideration of stamps. One cannot
imagine the majority of nations whose governments are always
doing those things which need plenty of justification neglect-
ing the opportunity for propaganda that the constant and
universal use of the postage stamp provides. In fact, this
opportunity has not gone neglected, and every day sees its use
confirmed and widened. And here it is proper to remark that
there is something which, though not a postage stamp (and
so, technically, outside the scope of our enquiry), is so closely
associated with it as to have no purpose or existence apart
from it: that is, the cancellation, which, like the postage stamp
itself, has passed beyond its original purely functional purpose
and has now assumed the form of a commentary upon the
idea incorporated in the design of the stamp itself. So far, the
"cancellation-legend" has been divided fairly evenly between
appeals to the public of the issuing country to perform some
meritorious act—Learn the Highway Code for instance—or
to the public of other lands to visit the country which makes
the appeal. As with the postage stamps that they cancel, these
legends have been, up to now, painstakingly innocuous:
perhaps more so than the stamps' designs in many cases.
During the last war the "solidarity" of the United Nations
was stressed in the wording of the legends, but now that peace
has come again, the wordings have reverted to their pre-war
inoffensiveness. Yet here is one more example of the manner
in which a mechanical process may be turned to the uses of
propaganda.

It is obvious that an international censorship came into
being with the perversion of the postage stamp into an
instrument of international message-carrying: a censorship
not the less strict because it has never been officially established or announced. But that it does exist is the reason why
stamps (and their cancelling legends) have so far remained
within what that cultured soul, the late Fuehrer, used to call

'the limits of good taste". And that the valuable opportunities for propaganda inherent in the stamp and its cancellation are regarded by governments as part of the not-to-be-infringed monopoly of the Ruler is evident from the late seizing, by the British Government, of letters bearing a "party" slogan issued by the Conservative Central Office. Though one may deplore monopoly and unnecessary governmental interference with the liberty of the subject, the writers feel that in this instance interference was justified: not because there was anything inherently offensive (save to Socialists) in the Conservative's slogan, but because any precedent of that sort is to be avoided, and the sooner that all stamps are as non-committally objective as those of Great Britain, and all cancellation marks revert to their original simplicity, the better for international relations as a whole.

It seems to the writers that, while the use of postage stamps as instruments of international propaganda will not decrease, the possibility of precipitating the refusal of foreign mail at the ports of entry will always make the avoidance of the cruder messages a *sine qua non* in preparing the design of even the boldest piece of stamp propaganda. That this simply means that the designer must concentrate not so much upon the truth as upon the subtle concealment of truth's exact opposite goes without saying. But it means also that a free-for-all, with "Gott Strafe England" cancelling out the German, "Workers of the World Unite", the Russian, and "Invite Britain into the Union", the U.S.A., appears to belong to the far-distant future, if, indeed, it belongs to the future at all. We feel that, long before the gloves were half-way off the fingers, nervous governments would prohibit international mails altogether.

For the future, then, we may expect to see—unless an international agreement puts the clock back to the days of 1850—a refinement, rather than an extension, of the present usage. Stamp designs and cancellation legends will continue to be "discreet", but more attention will be given to their propaganda-message, and whereas the propaganda to-day is spasmodic and discontinuous, in the future it will be as carefully conducted as an advertising campaign designed to sell

some patent shoe-polish or household soap, the success of such
a campaign depending, as most people know, upon the continuity of the message. Stamps, in future, expressly designed
for propaganda purposes, will not henceforward be designed
singly, but in groups, in which, even if "every picture tells a
story", the whole series will point the moral with unmistakable
plainness. Such a continuous series has already been inaugurated as publicity for Leipzig's Annual Trade Fair.

The writers foresee series of stamps issued in numbered
and carefully dated sections, each a significant part of an
organic whole. What a time the propagandists will have, in
conjunction with the designers, in making the best use of the
few square millimetres of brightly coloured paper! And what
a time the schoolboy of the future will have in endeavouring
to keep pace with the multitudinous outpourings from the
presses! The late unlamented Mr. Seebeck will seem un-
imaginative compared with the stamp propagandists of the
immediate future.

CHAPTER IX

Stories in Stamps

THE history of Philately is peculiarly rich in stories of treasure-trove, for the reason that, whereas the gold that treasure-seekers find was buried as gold, the treasure-trove which is unearthed to delight the hearts of philatelists went into hiding as something of perhaps no value at all: a stamp in a schoolboy's album, put away, with other childish things, fifty years before; a stamp on a letter getting dustier each year in a forgotten trunk; a stamp which was once used to form part of the decoration of a "scrap-work" fire-screen. Their value has grown with the years: the very neglect to which the years have condemned them has made them acquire a value which, when they are discovered, may well rival their weight in something much more costly than platinum.

Towards the end of 1903 a London civil servant, Mr. James Bonar, was going through some old papers, more with a view to indulging that sentimental desire to handle the material relics of the past happiness than to look for anything of more material value. Mr. Bonar, in the course of his turning over his papers, came across a sixpenny note-book that he recognised at once as having served as his stamp album when, as a schoolboy of nearly half a century earlier, he had—like most other schoolboys—been infected with the stamp-collecting craze.

Mr. Bonar left the note-book out when he returned the other papers to the drawer from which he had taken them: he intended to give it to his grandson, a lad who was due, Mr. Bonar reflected, to get the philatelic infection himself.

But that evening a family friend, a Miss D. Thomas, came to dinner, and because Miss Thomas knew something of the value of stamps, the note-book was produced and Miss Thomas's opinion asked on the worth of the little collection.

Idly Miss Thomas turned the pages, seeing only what she had expected to see, the valueless stamps that a schoolboy had acquired for a penny or a bird's egg or a bag of "conkers". Then—and it might happen to any one of us—the lady was looking in wonder at a perfect specimen of the 2d. "Post Office Mauritius".

Perhaps hardly daring to commit herself to an opinion in a matter so important to the fortunate schoolboy who had grown into an even more lucky man, Miss Thomas advised Mr. Bonar to seek the opinion of an established philatelic expert, and, acting on his friend's advice, Mr. Bonar called in the late Mr. Nevile Stocken, who has told the story in his memoirs with considerable detail and not a little dramatic effect. Mr. Stocken, too, was reluctant to commit himself to a snap-judgment, principally because of the superb condition of the stamp; nor until he had subjected it to the radical test of boiling—for the stamp had been gummed to a page of the note-book, and not affixed by the more classic method of a stamp-mount—could he feel himself free to inform Mr. Bonar that he was the happy possessor of the finest specimen of the 2d. "Post Office Mauritius" known.

The auction of the stamp at the Leicester Square Galleries, on January 13th, 1904, was an event which had received an immense amount of newspaper publicity. Dealers and philatelists from every part of the world were in attendance to watch or to bid at the sale of this pearl among stamps. It was an added piece of good fortune for Mr. Bonar that he was dissuaded from withdrawing the stamp from auction, after he had told the auctioneers, Messrs. Puttick & Simpson, that he wished to do so, as he had received a private offer of £1,000.

The bidding started at £500, and by hundreds the price rose to . . . £1,450, the stamp being knocked down to Mr. W. Crawford, acting on behalf of the then Prince of Wales, later King George V, in whose wonderful collection it was then enshrined.

Around the turn of the century several specimens of the Mauritius "Post Office" issue (Pl. XXIV) came to light, as people, learning that they were valuable, hunted through papers of half a century before, but none was so fortunate or—in the opinion of the writers—so deserving of his good fortune as the schoolboy who, inspired by reading a series of articles dealing with the "Post Office" stamps in a French philatelic journal, pestered his mother to let him go through the business papers of his dead father, who had been a *commerçant* of Bordeaux. Madame was none too keen to permit the lad to peruse letters which might well deal with matters too delicate to be entrusted to the immature discretion of a boy; but to youthful importunacy the young philatelist added not only the fanatic enthusiasm of a confirmed stamp-collector but the even more burning zeal of the treasure-hunter whose "divining" sense tells him of the nearness of success. In the end she gave her son permission to look through the correspondence of his dead father's firm, and for many a boring hour did he turn over the dusty papers, sustained in his effort only by a hope which seemed to grow less credible with every file which yielded nothing.

It was in his hunt in the last few papers remaining that his patience was magnificently justified: in a transport of joy the youth recognised, upon two letter-sheets which had been bound into the correspondence-file, no fewer than three of the stamps that he had set out to find. Of the two letter-sheets one was a rarity of rarities, for it not only bore a stamp of each value—1d. and 2d.—"Post Office Mauritius", but written directions and postal-cancellations on the cover marked the journey (and thus the authenticity) of the letter, from its posting in Port Louis, on October 4th, 1847, to its arrival— via Plymouth, Boulogne and Paris—at Bordeaux eighty-five days later. This envelope is unique, in that it is the only one known which bears a copy of each value of the "Post Office" issue.

It was to M. Th. Lemaire, the man whose articles on the Mauritius stamps had inspired the lad to search through his father's files, that these treasures were offered, and M. Lemaire —sensible man—did not refuse the stamps. For the letter bearing the 1d. and 2d. together M. Lemaire paid the equivalent of £1,600, for the letter which bears one copy of the 2d.

value he paid £1,200, so that the schoolboy had reason to congratulate himself, both on his "hunch" and on the assiduity with which he pursued his inspiration.

In 1922 the late Arthur Hind bought the letter bearing the two stamps for £7,500, though it is only just to add that when the Hind collection was sold in 1934 this item realised only £5,000, a rare case of a fall in value of a classic stamp. The other letter, bearing the 2d. "Post Office Mauritius", was bought by P. Kosack for the Reichpost Museum in Berlin, where let us hope it is still safe.

A unique item in the collection of the late Baron Erik Leijonhuvfud, the well-known Swedish diplomat and philatelist, was preserved as a "curiosity"—as so many unique or exceedingly rare stamps have been. A lady in Sweden, sending some jewels to London in 1867, used an entire sheet of the 20-ore value in order to frank the parcel. The London jeweller who received it preserved the wrapping of the parcel, and many years afterwards the Baron was gratified to acquire this certainly unique philatelic treasure for his world-famous collection.

*   *   *

The authors know of only one stamp which has been recovered from a river bed, and as not only the rarity of the stamp concerned but the curious circumstances of its loss and eventual recovery make a story as rare as the stamp, the circumstances are worth recalling.

The stamp was the most valuable of all Canadian issues: the "12d. Black" of 1851 (Pl. IV). The reason for the curious numeration is this: the Canadian currency of that day had depreciated in relation to the pound sterling, and fifteen pence in Canadian currency was asked for a shilling British.

Again, the term "shilling" was in use in various parts of North America, and signified—according to the district—any sum ranging from three-halfpence to ten pence. Had the denomination, then, been rendered "one shilling", considerable confusion would have resulted, to the detriment of the postal revenue. But "twelve pence" was completely unambiguous.

Ninety years ago an elderly Canadian occupied a small wooden house overlooking the St. Lawrence River. He had occasion to send by post some valuable deeds which had been entrusted to his care, and one evening he was busy making up the parcel when his ne'er-do-well nephew knocked at the door. The young man had—once again—been gambling, and now, upon his entering his uncle's parlour, followed the usual hard-luck story: the description of the gambler's troubles; the assurance that gambling was now a thing of the past; the humble request for the very last "loan" of all, to "clear things up".

The uncle's reply was as terse as to the point. He went back to the business upon which he was engaged when the nephew came in: stamped the envelope containing the deeds—with a "12d. Black"—and closed and locked the iron deed-box from which he had taken the documents now to be entrusted to the post.

Desperate for want of money, the young man made a grab for the deed-box, and in the struggle for its possession which followed the grab, the oil-lamp was overturned and the flimsy dwelling was soon blazing. With a final blow at his uncle's face, the worthless nephew bolted from the house, while, with a last rally of strength, the uncle threw the deed-box through the window into the waters of the St. Lawrence.

For more than forty years the box remained on the river-bed, and only the need to clear a channel in the St. Lawrence opposite the spot where the tragedy had taken place disturbed it. A powerful dredger was sent to the place, and one day a bulky object was seen to be caught in the teeth of one of the dredges. A member of the crew secured the object, which was, of course, the deed-box, its contents completely unharmed by forty years immersion in the water. The deeds were sent to their owner, and the man who rescued the box from the dredge was rewarded with a sum of money and the envelope in which the deeds had been enclosed. The 12d. stamp on that cover fetched £70 at auction in those days.

*   *   *

The late Mr. E. Stanley Gibbons, founder of the firm of philatelic dealers which bears his name, used often to tell a story of the days when he was still trading from his father's chemist shop in Plymouth, and Mr. C. J. Phillips, who was for many years chairman of Stanley Gibbons Ltd., recounts it thus, in his *Fifty Years of Philately*:

"One morning, two sailors, passing by the chemist's shop, noticed the sheets of stamps in one of the windows, and went inside and said: 'Do you buy used postage stamps?' On Mr. Gibbons replying in the affirmative, they said they had some on their ship and would bring them in. True enough, next day the men turned up, one of them carrying a kit-bag full of stamps over his shoulder.

"They were asked into the back-parlour, and turned out the contents of the bag on a table.

"The stamps were all triangular Capes, thousands and thousands of them, many in large strips and blocks of eight and more. Perkins, Bacon & Co.'s printings and 'woodblocks' were mixed up anyhow. Mr. Gibbons, even in those days, could not imagine how two sailors could have got a sackful of triangular Capes, and asked them for particulars.

"One of the men said: 'When our boat got to Cape Town, we had leave, and some of us went ashore for a spree; and me and my mate here happened to go into a show we found folks crowding into, and found a bazaar going on. Some ladies persuaded us to take a shilling ticket in a raffle, and we won this bag of stamps, which ladies had begged all round Cape Town for this bazaar.'

"The men were delighted to take a five-pound note for the lot, and departed highly pleased. Mr. Gibbons thought he made £500 and perhaps more out of this haul."

*   *   *

In 1912 the old-fashioned Philadelphia banking firm of Charnley & Whelan acquired a new partner in Mr. Townsend, who lived up to the proverbial qualities of new brooms by arranging to clear out a century's accumulation of old papers from deed-boxes, filing cabinets and vaults of the firm. He made contact with the Hemingway Paper Stock Company, who paid Mr. Townsend £10 for the "waste paper".

Apparently it was the custom of waste-paper merchants to sort their purchases before sending the paper to be pulped, and in this case it is as well that the Hemingway Paper Stock Company did so. For on old letters were found no fewer than one hundred and five St. Louis "Bears", together with a number of other early and rare U.S. issues. Altogether the stamps found fetched nearly one hundred thousand dollars. To-day they would be worth many times that sum.

This is the biggest find of St. Louis "Bears" to date; but, by one of those coincidences which are so common in the history of discovery that they excite no wonder, the genuineness of the St. Louis 20-cent was established by the finding of a large number of this issue, in circumstances which were almost duplicated by the find at Philadelphia seventeen years later.

Although the St. Louis stamps (Pl. XXI), which were one of the early U.S. issues, made on the initiative and by the authority of a local postmaster—whence their generic names of "locals" or "postmasters"—were known to the earliest philatelists and were mentioned in a catalogue of 1863, there were many who would not grant them a bona-fide character, and this in spite of the fact that one of the earliest (as well as one of the most famous) of our philatelists, the late Judge Philbrick, acquired a copy of the 5-cent in 1864. Mr. Philbrick, as he was then, was satisfied that his 5-cent St. Louis was genuine, but even he could not pronounce authoritatively upon the authenticity until, in the summer of 1895, a remarkable find put the matter of their genuine nature beyond all reasonable doubt. (In passing, Judge Philbrick's was one of the first "great" collections, and on his death was acquired by the late Herr Philippe la Renotière von Ferrari, for £7,000—a price which "made news" indeed, in those days.)

A coloured porter employed at the Louisville, Kentucky, court-house was told off to tidy up the cellars, and to burn an accumulation of old court records and general waste. The man was shovelling the papers into the lighted furnace, when some fell to the floor, and in picking them up he noticed that there were letters among them bearing unusual stamps. He put these letters aside, and added to them some others that he found in searching through the unburnt papers. When he came off duty, the porter showed the strange stamps to two caretakers employed in the building, and accepted a drink in return for the "curiosities". On the following day the caretakers came down into the cellar and made their own search through the papers which had been spared from the burning. In all, they found one hundred and thirty-seven stamps, all St. Louis "Bears", of the rarest variety: of the 20-cent, no fewer than sixteen copies; of the 10-cent, forty-six; and of the comparatively common 5-cent—for all that it is one of the world's rare stamps—seventy-five. These were not the days of the astronomical prices, but even with the relatively low price-standard obtaining in 1895, the lucky finders of this treasure netted, it is said, more than £4,000 for their haul. History, which is too often silent upon the really important details, does not say whether or not the negro porter received more than his one recorded drink.

*   *   *

Most of the best stamp stories centre, naturally, round that pipe-dream of every collector—the "fortunate find". Nor do these lucky strikes all belong to the past. They happen even in our own times.

It is a mistake, however, to think that philatelic treasures are to be sought and found only in forgotten deed-boxes or under the floors of old houses or anywhere in which something may lie neglected and undisturbed and, eventually, forgotten for many years. Mr. W. T. Robey, a stockbroker's clerk, of Washington, D.C., but a philatelist in his spare time, walked into the post office on May 14th, 1918, and there found a treasure which brought the fortunate clerk exactly $14,976 —a week after he had walked into the post office.

On May 14th a new U.S. stamp was due to be issued: an air-mail stamp, intended for use on the New York–Philadelphia–Washington air-route. Mr. Robey had an arrangement with some friends in New York, whereby he undertook to send them (and to receive from them in return) "first day covers", as they are called in the terminology of the philatelic fancy.

When, at last, Mr. Robey managed to slip away from the office, first of all to draw $30 from the bank, then to go to the nearest post office, he found that all but a few of the new stamps had been sold. "Come back at midday," said the post-office clerk, "and I shall have some more by then."

Mr. Robey returned at midday with his thirty dollars, and asked for his stamps. The post-office clerk produced a sheet, and offered it to Mr. Robey, when, in the stockbroker's clerk's own words, his "heart stood still".

And well might that organ have done, seeing that, on each stamp, the aeroplane shown in the centre *had been printed upside down.*

Now, although Mr. Robey earned his living in stock-broking, and not in printing, he knew, as an ardent philatelist, how such errors of typography come about. He knew, too, how exceedingly valuable they are in the eyes of philatelists, owing to the rarity that the close checks of postal officials make an essential quality of such errors.

He paid over his $24 for the entire sheet, and only then did he call the attention of the post-office clerk to the error, asking if, perchance, there might be other sheets. There were none, and the clerk went straight to the telephone, to advise his superiors of the error.

In the meanwhile Mr. Robey, like a prudent man, had left the post office with his treasure: a precaution upon which he had reason later to congratulate himself, when postal officials, at first with requests, then with bribes, and lastly with threats, endeavoured to persuade Mr. Robey to give up his sheet of "inverted air-mails".

Mr. Robey stuck to his find, and during the week following invited offers from the dealers. His first was for $500, but he sold eventually for $15,000, though a further offer of $18,000 —from the very dealer who had originally offered the five hundred!—had to be passed over, since the syndicate which bought the stamps for $15,000 already had an option. The entire sheet of one hundred stamps was then sold to Colonel

Green, a well-known American collector, for $20,000. The Colonel was persuaded to split the sheet, and since then the prices of single specimens have steadily risen, a copy fetching no less than $4,100 at the Stephen D. Brown sale in New York, on November 3rd, 1939.

* 　　　* 　　　*

There is a similar story, with its setting in North London, which may be added to the tale of Mr. Robey, in order to prove our point that philatelic treasures are not to be sought exclusively among the surviving relics of the past.

It was in June 1935 that the secretary of a North London stamp collector returned from the post office with some stamps that she had gone to buy. They were the ordinary 2½d. value, but the collector saw at once that the shade of the ink in which they had been printed differed substantially from the usual light tint of ultramarine: the stamps were in fact of the shade known as Prussian blue. He decided to investigate, and on enquiring at the post office, he found that three sheets in the darker colour had been received a day or two before, and that there were still some copies in stock. These the collector acquired—the remaining three hundred and nineteen out of an original three hundred and sixty.

The collector did not show, we are afraid, the business acumen of Mr. Robey in a similar position. A few of the "Prussian Blues" were sold to a local dealer, who disposed of all that he had at a shilling apiece; and a leading firm of stamp dealers, being offered the remainder, decided against buying after having "considered" the matter for some weeks.

Then the news of the strange stamp began to circulate, and when at last a firm of City dealers bought the stamps from the finder, they were soon disposing of copies at £40 each.

The three sheets which had gone to the Edmonton sub-post office were trial sheets, which had been distributed in error, and no more were found at other post offices. Of the forty-one that other persons had bought, thirteen (of which nine appear to have been destroyed) have been accounted for, so that there *may* still be twenty-eight to be found, and sold

at a handsome profit. One, which was on an envelope sent to
Holland, fetched £52 10s. at auction—a profit of no less than
504,000 per cent.

*   *   *

There are four apparently unique stamps in the world:
that is to say, stamps of which only one copy has, so far, come
to light, or of which only one copy is known to have survived.
These four stamps are: the 1-cent British Guiana, 1856 (there
is a strange story that another copy of this now unique stamp
was burnt by the late Arthur Hind, in order to preserve the
quality of uniqueness for the existing specimen); the Swedish
3-skilling-banco, yellow (error: it should have been blue),
1857; the 5-cent Boscawen Postmaster stamp, 1846; and the
1-mark Togo, overprinted "Occupation Franco-Anglaise",
1915. But of the four stamps, none has captured the popular
interest as has the "One Cent British Guiana" of 1856, though
we hesitate to say that that is because for some time it was
portrayed on the cover of the London Telephone Directory,
where it illustrated the advertisement of a famous firm
of stamp dealers.

In 1856, the supply of the regular issue of British Guiana
stamps having become exhausted, and replacements from
Waterlow's of London having been delayed, the Postmaster-
General of the colony decided to issue provisional stamps,
pending the arrival of stocks from Britain. The task of printing
these provisionals was entrusted to the firm of Baum & Dallas,
publishers of the Georgetown, Demerara, *Official Gazette,*
and, in the absence of means either for engraving or for litho-
graphing the provisional stamps, the firm set the design in
ordinary type, with a border of printer's rules, using for the
ship crest of the colony the somewhat crude cut of a schooner
which ordinarily headed the "Shipping Notes" article in the
Gazette (Pl. IV).

It is suspected that the "One Cent" is an error, but this has
not been proved, and certainly it bears the initials of E. D.
Wight, one of the postal officials who pen-marked the stamps,
owing to the fact that the postmaster of the colony thought so

poorly of their crude design that he feared that, unless each stamp was initialled by a responsible official, forgery might take place.

In 1873 Mr. L. Vernon Vaughan, of British Guiana, was a very small boy, but he had already started to collect stamps, and into his possession came what was afterwards believed to be the only known copy of the "One Cent British Guiana" of 1856. It is not a beautiful stamp, and young Vaughan wished dearly to exchange it for something prettier. He had recently had some approval sheets sent to him by an English dealer, and he was anxious to acquire some really beautiful stamps included in the approval sheets. He had found the "One Cent" among some family letters, and when he offered his rather poor specimen to a local collector, Mr. N. R. McKinnon, for six shillings, the boy was confident that he would be always able to find a better specimen among the family papers, where there were dozens of stamped envelopes. Mr. McKinnon did not betray the reputation associated with persons who bear such names as his: he bargained a good deal before parting with that six shillings. He told Vaughan that the stamp was in poor condition; that the edges should have been cut square, and not chamfered; that . . . well a lot of things. But when he learnt that young Vaughan wanted the cash in order to buy some brightly tinted stamps which had come all the way from England, Mr. McKinnon's collector's heart softened, and he handed the boy the money with these words, which well deserve to become immortal: "Now, look here, my lad, I'm taking a great risk in paying so much for this stamp, and I hope you'll appreciate my generosity!"

Five years later McKinnon sold his collection, through a Glasgow friend, Wylie Hill. There were two bidders for it, but Thomas Ridpath, of Liverpool, secured the collection by taking the train to Glasgow, where his rival was content to send a cheque by post. Ridpath paid £120 for the entire collection McKinnon had made, and the "One Cent British Guiana" he sold to Philippe la Renotière von Ferrari, the world-famous Austrian philatelist, for—it is said— approximately £150.

PLATE XVII

Frank Godden Ltd.

MAPS IN MINIATURE

Venezuela-Guiana Boundary Dispute, 1896; San Domingo-Haiti Boundary
Dispute, 1900; Imperial Penny Postage Scheme, 1898; Irish Republic,
1922; Falkland Islands Dependencies, 1946; Argentina Republic, 1936

PLATE XVIII

GERMAN STAMPS

Rise of the German Empire; Weimar Republic, and after; flight from the Mark; Hindenburg regime; reoccupation of the Rhineland; first Nazi "Putsch"; Adolf Hitler; return of the Saar

Only after the stamp had passed into the fabulous Ferrari collection did the philatelic world begin to realise that the wealthy collector had got, not something merely very rare, but something almost certainly unique.

The Ferrari collection, housed in a splendid mansion in the Rue Varennes, was probably the greatest which has ever been formed, for La Renotière von Ferrari was an extremely wealthy man, and by investing large sums in the acquisition not only of single specimens but also of entire collections he did more than anyone else to "boost" the international financial value of stamps, and to raise stamp collecting from the status of boy's hobby to that of the rich man's interest. Herr von Ferrari purchased the late Judge Philbrick's collection for £7,000; that of the late Sir Daniel Cooper, first President of the Philatelic Society, for £3,000, and the Thornhill collection of Australians for a considerably larger sum. It is to this heavy expenditure of von Ferrari's on stamps that we may attribute the fact that a specialised collection of Europeans, formed by Mr. M. P. Castle, M.V.O., J.P., could fetch £30,000 as early as 1899.

But to return to the Ferrari collection and the British Guiana stamp that he had acquired. When, in 1914, war broke out between France and Austria, von Ferrari fled to Lausanne, leaving his collection behind him in the Rue Varennes. In 1917 von Ferrari died in Lausanne, and by his will he left his wonderful collection to the Imperial Reichpost Museum, in Berlin.

Unfortunately for the Reichpost Museum, Germany lost the war, and the French government, with a pettiness that some people will think not untypical of the Gallic bureaucrat, decided to sell the Ferrari collection and apply the proceeds to the reduction of the German reparations account!

The sale was effected in fourteen sessions, all taking place at the Hôtel Drouot, and lasting over a period of more than four years. Altogether, the sum of £400,000 was raised: a a figure which could easily have been doubled—or even trebled—had the stamps been sold in smaller quantities, and over a longer period.

8*

The "high spot" of the sale was undoubtedly the "One Cent British Guiana" of 1856, a stamp which, during the time that it had lain in the Ferrari collection, had received the authentic *cachet* of uniqueness.

On April 6th, 1922, the attention of the whole stamp world was fixed on the duel which opened between M. Maurice Burrus, a Mulhaus tobacco king, and a London dealer, the late Mr. Hugo Griebert, who was bidding on behalf of an American plush-manufacturer, the late Arthur Hind. It is said that the price which was eventually paid for the stamp by Mr. Griebert—the hitherto unequalled sum of £7,343— could easily have been doubled had not a misunderstanding over a bid occurred, and had not M. Burrus most generously conceded the final bid to Mr. Griebert.

The last word on this stamp must come from its first owner, Mr. Vernon Vaughan himself. The price fetched by the stamp that he had once sold for six shillings had made it "news" in other circles than purely philatelic ones. Mr. Vaughan wrote an article entitled, "The Rarest Stamp Once Belonged to Me", in the course of which he said this:

" . . . the world's greatest stamp dealers and philatelists are ready to outbid each other and pay ridiculous sums of money for that little scrap of paper that I once owned. Really, it does seem remarkable! People ask me what I feel about it. . . . As a matter of fact, I hardly ever think of it at all now, and never with disappointment or chagrin. What is the use?"

*   *   *

It was in British Guiana that another remarkable find of early stamps was made: this time stamps of the sort known to philatelists as "Cotton-reels", from their resemblance to the circular pieces of paper which are stuck on the ends of cotton-spools. For her Easter-offering to Christ Church, Georgetown, of which she was a member, an elderly coloured lady, Miss Preston, sent to the incumbent, the Ven. Archdeacon Josa, a pair of 4-cents deep blue of 1856, which were sold for the comparatively small sum of $33.60. On Easter Monday, Archdeacon Josa went to thank his generous parishioner, and casually enquired, when he had arrived at her house, if she had any more old stamps—for the affairs of Christ Church were somewhat embarrassed financially, and the clergyman had a large debt to meet on the school.

"Miss Preston said she had given all her stamps away [the Archdeacon relates], but she brought out an old basket filled with old receipts and bills—and I searched; when lo! and behold there tumbled out of the basket an envelope addressed:

Miss Rose,

BLANKENBURG.

this being the name of one of our plantations on the West Coast of Demerara. This envelope contained two stamps, an unsevered pair, cut to shape, and they were the very stamps that buyers had been in search of, and for which there were standing advertisements."

It happened that Miss Rose, the lady to whom the envelope had been addressed forty-five years earlier, was in the room. On hearing that the two stamps were worth a lot of money, she literally danced with joy, and said: "Thank God! I am at last able to give something worth while!"

The church profited to the extent of £205, and the dealer who bought the envelope—the only known pair of the "Cotton-reel" 2-cents of 1850—sold it immediately for £600 to the well-known London firm of Stanley Gibbons. At the Hind sale in 1934 the same envelope fetched £1,300.

*   *   *

There is not space within the covers of a normal-sized book, let alone within the limits of a single chapter, to recount half the tales of treasure-trove that one may find in the annals of Philately: but not all those tales have happy endings, and some of them, though of wide currency and of astonishing hardihood, are not true. We have space here only to mention one example of each kind.

With regard to the hardy fable, perhaps the one best known to stamp collectors concerns The Miner From The Far North, who walked into the shop of a Vancouver stamp dealer, and told the dealer that he had two stamps, found among his dead father's papers, which had been rejected by the post office. The postal clerk had suggested that the stamp dealer might be interested: was he? The "old stamps" were a mint pair of "12d. Black Canada", 1851.

There are many picturesque details in this story, whose perfectly classic form insists upon the mention of the shabby purse from which The Miner drew forth the philatelic treasure.

Now, the proof of this picturesque tale's unreality lies in the fact that it finds a final resting place for the mint pair of "12d. Blacks" in the collection of the late Alfred Lichtenstein, and the origin of Mr. Lichtenstein's pair of "12d. Blacks" is established beyond all question. They turned up, not in Vancouver, but in Victoria, the capital city of the province of British Columbia, which is situated on Vancouver Island, and the dealer who handled the purchase for Mr. Lichtenstein was Mr. Ronald M. Angus, of Victoria, to whom we are indebted for a full account of what really happened in this matter of Mr. Lichtenstein's "12d. Blacks". The truth is hardly less romantic than the fiction, for the stamps had been cut from the corner of a sheet by a postal employee at the time that Canada changed over from a pence to a cents currency: this man had clipped them off as a memento of the change. On his death, sixty-eight years later, his heirs found them in a safe-deposit in the Belmont Building, Victoria, and five years later Mr. Angus acquired a pair for Mr. Lichtenstein.

Mr. Angus tells us that he has put the whole transaction upon record in a philatelic journal, but knowing the astonishing survival value of such hardy perennials as the tale of The Miner From The Far North, we doubt that twenty such articles would kill it.

*   *   *

A tragic tale of The Treasure Which Might Have Been is, on the other hand, a true one, and is quoted from the brothers L. N. and M. Williams's delightful *More Famous Stamps*, a mine of philatelic lore.

There are two valuable stamps of Naples: the half-tornese blue, one bearing the triple arms of Naples, Sicily and the Bourbon dynasty—hence this stamp's nickname of "Trinacria"—and the other having the white cross of the House of Savoy replacing the earlier Bourbon armorial bearings. Now the half-tornese—both "Trinacria" and "Savoy Provisional"—were used mostly for newspaper postage, and as the wrappers of newspapers are not preserved as are envelopes, these stamps have become exceedingly rare—and correspondingly valuable.

A Neapolitan collector remembered that a friend of his, an artist, had been a subscriber to a number of journals at the time when the half-tornese stamps were in issue, and the collector asked his friend if, perchance, he had retained the wrappers in which the journals had been sent?

No, the artist replied, he had not kept the wrappers. Only the stamps which had been on them.

"Do you collect stamps, then?"

No, the artist did not collect stamps, but the blue colour of the half-tornese stamps attracted him, and he used those which had been removed from the wrappers in order to decorate the top of a small table.

"And where is the table now?" the collector asked, his heart in his mouth.

No, it had not been lost or given away. It was in an upstairs storeroom to which it had been sent some time before. The artist offered to send the maid to bring it down.

He rang for the maid, and asked her to fetch the table. Alas! The table was there, but not the hundreds of "Trinacrias" and their Savoyard successors. The girl explained she had tried to wash the stamp-covered table-top, which had become soiled with use. Warm water and soft soap, however gently applied, soon removed the stamps, so—"I thought it would be best—as I could do no better—to clean it off altogether, and now the wood is quite plain as it was originally, and looks much nicer like that!"

As the authors of *More Famous Stamps* rightly remark, "the feelings of the artist, and more so those of the collector, can be better imagined than described', and they add that "there is no doubt that the 'Trinacria' would be a commoner stamp to-day had it not been for that act of unconscious vandalism".

*   *   *

Nor can the days of philatelic "finds" be regarded as over. Every now and again some sensational discovery of unsuspected wealth causes a nine-day wonder, and not infrequently makes the headlines. Little more than twenty years ago a London lady of title came across an old portfolio belonging to her grandfather, which had lain unopened for close upon half a century. He had been a great traveller in his day, and with uncanny foresight had bought stamps at the local post office wherever he went, not in single copies as was customary in those days, but almost always in full post-office sheets. Therein lay the particular value of the so-called "Mayfair Find", for it enabled connoisseurs of rare stamps to acquire some of the finest examples in larger "pieces" than had hitherto been known to exist. The accumulation, for it could not rightly be deemed a "collection", was dispersed at auction, where it realised many thousands of pounds.

Under somewhat similar circumstances a unique block of the first twopenny stamp of Great Britain came to light in an old writing-case used by one of the former Dukes of Buccleuch. In its pristine state it sold readily for £5,000.

Most costly of all British stamps is the ten-shilling denomination of the King Edward VII series overprinted with the legend "I.R.OFFICIAL" for exclusive use on correspondence of the Department of Inland Revenue (Pl. V). A single copy in mint condition is catalogued at £2,000. Up to 1947 no more than thirteen such examples were known, and a very inferior specimen which came on to the market in 1938 had fetched only £375. On a spring day in 1947 a large cardboard box filled with stamps of all kinds was handed in at a Strand auction room, with an enquiry whether they were worth putting up for sale. Most of the contents proved to be of very little value, but on opening up a small jeweller's box enclosed with the rest, the valuer was amazed to come across no fewer than nine of the rare ten-shilling stamps, joined together in one piece. True, they had been rolled up and were rather creased and dishevelled, though admittedly unused, and this detracted from their philatelic worth. Nevertheless, after being pressed out and improved, as far as possible, this unique block was ultimately bought by a leading firm of London stamp dealers for £4,000.

A stroke of luck such as can happen but once in a lifetime befell a certain stamp dealer a short time ago. When special stamps were created by the British Post Office to celebrate the holding in London of the Olympic Games of 1948, a proportion was surcharged with equivalent denominations in Indian currency for sale by our postal agencies in Southern Arabia. Checking over a batch of sheets which he was about to break up for distribution in a new-issue service, he came across one on which, through a printer's error, on each of the 120 stamps the words "1 RUPEE" had been printed twice (Pl. XXIV), thus constituting one of the major forms of philatelic error and, at the same time, raising the saleable value of the stamps from six to several thousand pounds. And it could happen to you!

So the always fascinating tale of stampic treasure-trove might be continued *ad infinitum*.

*   *   *

In conclusion, then, let us say that while even some of the most valuable "finds" have been made by persons with little or no specialised philatelic knowledge, the recognition of the "find's" value has been made only by persons possessing such knowledge. Mr. Bonar, in whose boy's album the "King's Copy" of the 2d. "Post Office Mauritius" was found, had had the stamp for forty years, and would have given it to his grandson had not a friend of his family, Miss Thomas, to whom he was idly showing his little collection, recognised— out of her superior philatelic knowledge—the treasure for what it was.

In his excellent handbook, *Stamp-Collecting*, Mr. Richard Curle tells a story which well emphasises the dependence of discovery upon expert knowledge: a dependence which is by no means confined to the discovery of rare stamps. "For example," says Mr. Curle, "an acquaintance of mine, seeing a common Swedish stamp, the 3-ore of 1862, on an envelope, happened to recall that very occasionally this stamp is found printed, by mistake, also on the back, and so thought it just worth his while to soak it off and have a glance. Sure enough, it *was* printed on the back, which raised the price from about 6d. to about £75. But how many of us would have had the flair to do this?"

The answer is: very few. And the significant words in Mr. Curle's tale are these: "He happened to recall . . . "— the moral being, of course, that it is useless to look for treasures if the seeker lacks the ability to recognise them when he sees them.

Perhaps just one more story may be permitted, if only because it is a case of "the biter bit". A rather knowing-looking youth walked into a down-town stamp shop in New York, and said to the dealer, "Hey, mister, this stamp I got from you yesterday—there seems to be something wrong with it." Now there is a very rare variety of the 30-cents U.S. stamp of 1869 (Pl. IV) which has the flags on either side of the coat of arms printed, accidentally, upside down; and this was one of them! Wise in his generation, the dealer replied "Yes, son, there does appear to be something wrong. Would you rather I changed it?" "Sure," said the boy, "give me some of those Guatemalans with parrots on them." Nothing loth, the exchange was effected, but on reaching the door, the Smart Alec stopped to call out, "I had you there, mister; that stamp never came from you, I took it out of my Pop's old album", and beat a hasty retreat—leaving the dealer to gloat over his lucky break.

CHAPTER X

Stamps that have Altered History

T HAT postage stamps record historic events is a truth so obvious as to seem almost trite, but that a stamp may have—has, indeed, had—the power to influence the trend of happenings, often in a radical and highly dramatic fashion, may not be so easily accepted by those who have not studied the history of Philately. Yet it is so: and not only the careers of politicians and soldiers, but the fortunes of governments—of nations themselves—have been affected, mostly adversely, by the small oblongs of tinted paper, still regarded by many as objects worthy only of the attention of idle schoolboys.

For instance, the first stamps of Korea have much to do with the eventual seizure of that country by the Japanese, whose imperialism was always excused by the "need to restore order" in the lands that they coveted. It was not long after Japan's "awakening" that she was very wide awake indeed—a Great Power, and as hungry for conquest as all Great Powers usually are.

Her eyes first fell on Korea, nominally under Chinese suzerainty, but in effect completely independent. Korea had (for the Japanese) the inestimable advantages of being easily accessible from the Japanese mainland while being hard of access from other lands; of being "backward", i.e. not possessed of modern weapons; and of being internally unsettled.

It was in 1882 that, by Japanese advice, Korea emerged from her isolation, made treaties of friendship and commerce with the Western Powers, and two years later inaugurated a postal system, the stamps and necessary postal equipment being supplied by Tokyo.

A post-office building was erected in Seoul, the capital, and on December 4th, 1884, a banquet was held in the new building, to mark both the completion of the edifice and the inauguration of Korea's postal system. Stamps of five values had been ordered from Tokyo. By the night of the party, however, only two of the values had been delivered in Seoul: the 5 and 10 moon (Pl. XXI).

But there was a Progressive Party in Korea: marked, as most such parties usually are, by a fierce nationalism, which found itself deeply offended by the growing power of the Japanese over the Korean king and government.

They, too, were looking for an excuse; and the Japanese-printed stamps and the Japanese-sponsored and designed post-office provided it.

That night, as the guests sat at their dinner in the new post-office building, the Progressives made a bid to seize power. They made first of all for the hated post office, which had come to symbolise, in the eyes of the revolutionaries, every detestable quality in the government that they sought to overthrow. First, they attempted to assassinate the king's agent, who staggered into the banqueting hall with blood flowing from a dozen wounds. The new building they looted, scattering the sheets of stamps through the gutters of Seoul. Then they burnt it. For three days the mob held the capital, plundering, murdering, burning, until at last order was restored by the Japanese and Chinese troops.

It had been the very opportunity that the Japanese had looked for. From that moment Korean independence was doomed.

*   *   *

Just as radically affecting the fate of a nation were the stamps issued by the Republic of Nicaragua for the years 1900, 1901 and 1902; all showing the volcano Mt. Momotombo in an obviously active condition, with sulphurous smoke pouring densely from the crater.

Now Ferdinand de Lesseps, the French engineer who had successfully reopened the ancient canal through the Isthmus of Suez, had undertaken to cut another across the Isthmus of Panama, but the fevers of the Panamanian swamps had proved too much for his workers, and, after an enormous amount of capital had been sunk in the work, the French engineers regretfully had to declare themselves beaten by nature.

A decade passed, and with it came a scientific comprehension of "fevers": of their cause and their combating. The engineering problems connected with the making of the canal presented no insuperable difficulties; and now that medical research had shown the way to keep the workers healthy in a fever-ridden land, there was no reason why a further attempt to cut the canal should not be made . . . and should not be successful.

The French had no desire to make that second attempt: the first attempt had not only been excessively costly in cash and men, but had produced a political scandal of the first magnitude; so that the very name "Panama" stank in the nostrils of a nation. Again, in the decade between the abandoning of the canal-cutting and the close of the Spanish-American War, the United States had reaffirmed its own interpretation of the Monroe Doctrine, and—as a corollary of that interpretation—had established the Pan-American Union. It was, then, inevitable that the United States should look upon the cutting of the Atlantic–Pacific canal as both the duty and the prerogative of the Big Brother of the Pan-American Union.

The French company had agreed to sell its rights and equipment for the equivalent of eight millions sterling. The business of selling the rights of the bankrupt company to Washington had been placed in the extremely capable hands of a certain Philippe Bunau-Varilla, formerly chief engineer for the French canal company.

M. Bunau-Varilla was in Washington when the board of engineers, recruited from many countries to report on the relative suitability of the Panama and Nicaragua sitings for the canal—for it was at first intended to be an international affair, though controlled by the United States—issued their report in favour of the former: a recommendation that it seemed likely the U.S. Senate would accept.

But—fortunately for M. Bunau-Varilla's ambitions— the entire Caribbean area was shaken with earthquakes: Mont Pelée, in Martinique, erupted violently, and an estimated forty thousand persons perished. Not long afterwards, Mt. Momotombo, which is situated at the westerly end of lake Managua, also burst into volcanic activity, and the earthquake which followed the eruption destroyed a large portion of the docks at Corinto, which would have been at the port-of-entry of the proposed Nicaraguan canal.

M. Bunau-Varilla had learnt the wisdom of taking time by the forelock: he bought sufficient copies of the Nicaraguan stamp which showed Mt. Momotombo, and pasting each one on a sheet of paper, he wrote beneath the stamp: "Postage stamp of the Republic of Nicaragua". Below that legend he wrote, "An official witness of the volcanic activity of Nicaragua" (Pl. XXI), going on then to give details of the volcano's activity and of the damage that the docks of Corinto had suffered. He added that the docks were identical with those shown in the stamp, where the smoking mountain looms menacingly above them. Senators sympathetically inclined towards Panama as a site for the proposed canal saw to it that the members of the pro-Nicaraguan party found a copy of M. Bunau-Varilla's statement on their desks before the Senate voted for a final decision. As we know, the Senate decided in favour of Panama, but how near Nicaragua came to being chosen as the site may be understood when it is recorded that had only four formerly pro-Nicaraguan senators not changed their minds, the Panama Canal would never have been completed.

*   *   *

Our next story takes us across the Pacific, to a part of the world which, though it has recently been much in the news, is little more known to the general public to-day than it was when Marie David de Mayrena became king: the hinterland of Annam, where live the Sedangs, the tribe of which De Mayrena became king.

It was in the eighties of the last century that De Mayrena assumed the crown of this primitive state, but he had lived for many years in the Far East, and his acquaintance with the Oriental character seems to have fitted him admirably for the duties of kingly rule. At all events, his reign was characterised by considerable social progress: treaties of commerce and friendship were signed with neighbouring tribes, and the export trade of the country was carefully fostered by this energetic and enlightened monarch, whose efforts on behalf of his adopted country were recognised by the French government to the extent that De Mayrena's royal rank was officially admitted by the land-hungry gentlemen of the Quai d'Orsay: no mean testimony to "King Marie's" qualities, for all this happened at the time of the great European scramble for colonies, and the "Powers" did not welcome amateur competition in the glorious game of land-grabbing!

King Marie having been "recognised", like the wolf in the fable the French government had to look around for an excuse to withdraw the "recognition" and to sacrifice poor King Marie's efforts and ambitions to the stern demands of *Realpolitik*. And, of course—as always happens in life—the lamb was not long in providing the excuse for action on the wolf's part.

In order to provide revenue for his infant state without having to adopt the always unpopular method of taxation, King Marie had commissioned a Parisian printing firm to prepare a series of stamps, "emblazoned with the royal arms, comprising a shield bearing a lion rampant, crossed swords and the inevitable crown" (Pl. IV).

This issue of postage stamps provided the necessary excuse, since the French government affected to see in King Marie's action a decision to set up a rival to the French authority in a part of the world that French arms was "pacifying" so energetically that the writer Pierre Loti, then a serving officer in the French navy, got himself suspended from active service by the indignant protests that he made against the savagery of the "peaceful penetration" of Indo-China.

"Recognition" of De Mayrena was solemnly withdrawn, and from having accorded him the respect due to an established royal rank, the French government now denounced the luckless king as an impostor.

It was in the spring of 1889 that King Marie the First of the Sedangs, glittering with orders, vouched for by the

French Consul, received by the Governor, arrived in Hong-Kong to become the lion of the colony.

It was two years later that another Frenchman, James D. Harden-Hickey, Baron of the Holy Roman Empire, landed with a companion on the island of Trinidad, a lifeless rock, some five miles in length and two in breadth, which lies seven hundred miles due east of Brazil. This Trinidad—not to be confused with a larger and more famous island of the same name—is an island composed of a porous volcanic rock, affording conditions of subsistence only to thousands of gulls and land-crabs; but men had come to it because of a legend, apparently by no means unsupported by excellent evidence, that at some time during the first quarter of the nineteenth century, a vast treasure had been buried on Trinidad. Within twelve years no fewer than five well-equipped expeditions went to dig for gold. But the last and quite the best equipped of these expeditions, that organised by Mr. E. F. Knight, made so good a job of the treasure-hunt as effectively to prove that what he could not find was, if not non-existent, then certainly unfindable by any other seeker.

In February 1890, Mr. Knight, with his disappointed company, left Trinidad for ever, and in the following year Baron James Harden-Hickey turned up, with his friend and "Chancellor", Count de la Boissière.

The Baron was on a British steamer, making a trip around the world, when the vessel on which he was travelling touched in at uninhabited Trinidad for water. Apparently under the impression that, though Mr. Knight had abandoned the treasure-hunt, the Peruvian gold was still findable by a luckier seeker, Harden-Hickey insisted upon being put ashore, and on his return to the ship solemnly claimed the island for his own.

Two years passed, during which the Baron and his "Chancellor" must have been drawing up the constitution of the new principality, for it was not until 1893 that, in a circular letter addressed to the Powers, Harden-Hickey proclaimed himself ruler of the independent sovereign state of Trinidad, with the style of Prince James the First. There is no evidence that the "proclamation" was ever acknowledged, though, as we shall see, there is evidence that it went by no means unrecorded. In spite of this snubbing by rulers longer-established, Prince James continued with his self-chosen task of organising his principality. As living conditions on Trinidad were hardly up to European standards—the giant crabs and sea-gulls menaced the visitor at every step!—Count de la Boissière established his Chancellory at New York, taking an office in Thirty-sixth street, from which address "le Grand Chancelier" informed the world that the arms of the . principality were "d'or, chapé de gules"; that the royal standard was a yellow triangle on a red ground, and that the first settlers would comprise, *de jure*, the aristocracy. For himself, the Prince reserved a monopoly of the guano, the turtles and the buried treasure, but his subjects-to-be were encouraged to dig for the treasure by the promise of a liberal percentage of the find. An order of chivalry was established, to "reward his subjects for prominence in literature, the arts and the sciences". A crown was ordered of a prominent firm of New York jewellers. All the same, the trivia of government alone did not engage the Prince's whole attention: he established an agent on the island, even though he could not himself face the prospect of enduring the rigours of its climate and the attacks of its inhabitants; and the construction of a harbour was begun.

Now so far the story of Baron James Harden-Hickey, first Prince of Trinidad, is that of a romantically minded schoolboy "playing at kings"; but, just as David de Mayrena had discovered a year or two earlier, even petty princes and kinglets of the most modest rank find themselves in company as resentfully jealous of its privileges as it is exalted in status. To sup with the devil, one needs a long spoon. And both David de Mayrena and his compatriot, James Harden-Hickey, lost their "thrones" through a naïve (and quite understandable) desire to cash in on the philatelic aspect of kingship. In October 1894 the first stamps of Trinidad appeared, beautifully printed, as most such issues are. The values were of 5, 10, 25, 50 and 75 centimes, and 1 franc and 5 francs. Coloured—respectively—

green, brown, blue, orange, mauve, red and grey, all bore the inscription, *Principauté de Trinidad—Timbre-Poste et Fiscal* (Pl. IV), and in connection with these stamps (and also in connection with the considerable doubts of their authenticity that their appearance provoked) Count de la Boissière wrote to the *Monthly Journal*, under date of April 1895, pointing out that "the financial personal condition of the Prince . . . removes every suspicion that his enterprise be destined to cover some speculation not owned to."

In spite, however, of their equivocal nature—or maybe because of it—the stamps sold well, at about $2 a set; but such financial advantage as accrued to the "Prince" through the sale of his stamps was poor compensation for the immense harm that the issue wrought to his adventure. For the stamps received considerable publicity, and the British Foreign Office, which had ignored the Prince's 'proclamation' of his little kingdom, now took his ambitions most seriously indeed. A cable was being laid from England to Brazil, and disregarding the fact that Trinidad was an 'independent sovereign state', the British government seized the island as a cable station.

The Prince was horrified: he instructed his Minister of Foreign Affairs—Count de la Boissière—to address a strong protest to all the Powers: but all of them treated the letter as did Richard Olney, the U.S. Secretary of State, who said that he was unable to read the handwriting, and turned it over to the Washington journalists as the communication of a crank. Poor Harden-Hickey did not survive this blow to his hopes and his pride, and three years after the seizure—in July 1895—of his little state, he shot himself in an El Paso hotel.

*　　　　　*　　　　　*

There are two stamps which, in the opinion of the authors, have had a remarkable effect upon modern history, though it is only fair to admit that our view is not universally supported. These stamps form part of that issue of 1906 which was prepared by the Imperial Austro-Hungarian government for use in the provinces of Bosnia and Herzegovina, which

PLATE XIX

Frank Godden Ltd.

ITALIAN STAMPS

"Trinacria" into "Savoy Cross", Naples; Kingdom of Italy, 1862; Humbert I, 1879; Victor Emmanuel III, 1901 *et seq.*; Rome-Berlin Axis; Italian Social Republic; Allied Military Government; Republic of Italy

PLATE XX

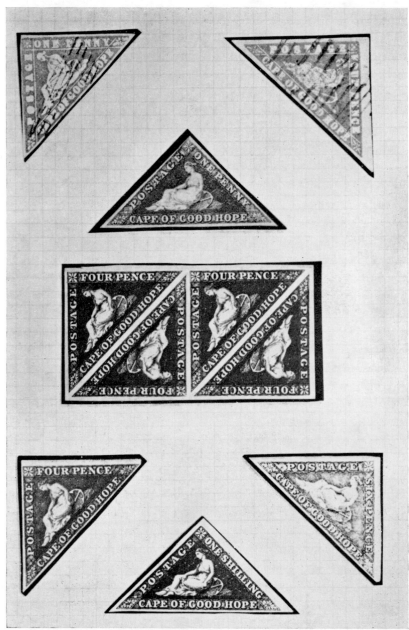

H. R. Harmer Ltd.

Issued just a hundred years ago (September 1853), these unconventional stamps of the Cape of Good Hope at once caught the fancy of collectors, so that to-day they are accounted among the "gilt-edged securities" of the stamp market.

Those in the top corners belong to the rare emergency printing made in Cape Town and erroneously described as "Wood-blocks" had been administered by Austria-Hungary since 1878, though they were nominally still part of the Turkish Empire.

When it became obvious to the Austro-Hungarian government that Turkey, as then organised, was due to be forced back into Asia Minor, and that Russia—through her satellites —would then control, not only the Dardanelles, but the southern Adriatic also, Vienna determined to effect the complete annexation of Bosnia and Herzegovina, and—just as Venezuela had done, ten years earlier—the Imperial Austrian Government used a postage stamp in order to prepare the world for an about-to-be-accomplished fact.

Accordingly, a well-designed pictorial issue appeared in 1906; and two years later the fact which had been promised —or threatened—by the issue of 1906 took place: Bosnia and Herzegovina were annexed by the Austro-Hungarian Empire.

Now the 45-heller and the 1-kroner designs had shown views of the ancient city of Sarajevo; and both for Austrians and for Serbs this city, capital of Bosnia, had an immense historical significance: which was why it was represented upon the stamps of 1906.

Very well, then: Austria annexed Bosnia and Herzegovina, and Tsarist Russia, by recognising the annexation, seemed to have betrayed her Slav cousins of what we now call Yugoslavia. The Serbs decided upon measures even more drastic than those which had made the Adriatic provinces of the Austro-Hungarian Empire so thorny a problem for the Imperial Chancellory.

The Crown Prince, Francis Ferdinand, had an ambition. He wished to appease these unwilling Austrian subjects. He planned a Balkan Union, with almost complete autonomy: but under the suzerainty of Austria, rather than that of Russia or Turkey.

This did not suit the books of the Slav irredentists: only complete freedom from Austrian control was their wish, and they saw in the Archduke Francis Ferdinand's plan nothing but the death-blow to their hopes of independence. So it was to ancient, historically memorable Sarajevo, capital of Bosnia, that the Archduke Francis Ferdinand and his wife went, to

9

mark, as it were, the official opening of the new plan for Slav pacification; and it was ancient Sarajevo that the desperate enemies of all things Austrian chose for the final, irremediable act of separation. On June 28th, 1914, the assassin Princip shot the royal couple, with what results we only too tragically know. Exactly one calendar month later, Austria declared war on Serbia (Pl. XXI).

His Imperial Highness would have been shot in any case . . . ? Not improbably. But we must bear in mind that it is most probable that it was because he came to Sarajevo that he was shot: had he stayed in Vienna, neither the opportunity nor, indeed, the necessity for his assassination would have come about. For Serbian aspirations had taken ancient Sarajevo as a symbol, because Austrian imperialism had already taken it as a symbol; and it was the stamp issue of 1906 which made that dangerous fact abundantly clear.

If there is a moral to be extracted from these representative stories, it must be that the potential for mischief which appears to reside in a stamp (that is to say, in its design) is afforded an opportunity for expression less by intention than by accident: that the stamp has, in other words, a vast influence upon public opinion, but rarely one which was aimed for by its designers. And, to sum up, it does seem to be established by the evidence that the only "safe" stamps are those which bear simply the name of the issuing state, together with only enough wording and figuring to identify their purpose and to indicate their value. For even the harmless digit may be charged with a dangerous political potential: "49" once had, in Britain, an immense political significance, and republics which enjoy the benefits of frequent—and forcible—changes of government always attach great value to the date of the last revolution. For instance, a stamp watermarked with the figures "175" would be most unacceptable to all but the dissatisfied elements of the Bolivian Republic, for the reason that, since the revolution May 17th, 1936, there has been another revolution, that of December 20th, 1943. Again, until Mussolini adopted the lictoral fasces as the emblem of his own totalitarian rule, this ancient Roman symbol of the civic authority was widely used, and, indeed, may be seen on a Swiss stamp of 1925. To-day, of course, the fasces has become so closely identified with Fascism that none but a declared Fascist state would dare to use the symbol, and even then prudence might counsel its non-employment.

Indeed, the ideal stamp is of such a design as was used by the Mexican government in 1884, which merely bore the value numeral, the value in words, and the legend "Mexican Postal Service". Or, even better, of the design used by the Brazilian government between 1843 and 1854, which, on an engine-turned background, bore simply the value-numerals (Pl. XXIII). Only with a stamp of so basic a simplicity of design may a state feel really safe from the dangers of offending the prejudices of others: prejudices, alas, whose presence is never suspected until they have unwittingly been offended.

CHAPTER XI

Some Strange Stamp Stories

WHEN Marshal Tito, Dictator of Yugoslavia, ordered a servile "government" to depose the young King Peter, and to declare the Kingdom of the Serbs, Croats and Slovenes a Soviet Republic, there was much sympathy for the deposed king. Under Peter, Yugoslavia had turned from an alliance with Germany and had espoused the cause of the allies: an act of desperate courage which was paid for with bitter suffering. Most people felt that fate had been cruelly unkind to the young king; but there is this of comfort in the deposition of King Peter: the affair was conducted with none of that world-shocking savagery with which, forty-two years ago, the House of Obrenovitch was overthrown, and the House of Karageorgevitch restored to the throne of Serbia, in the person of King Peter's grandfather, Peter I.

On the night of June 10th/11th, 1903, a group of army officers burst into the royal palace at Belgrade, and sabred the king, Alexander I, and his morganatic wife, Draga, as they lay sleeping. Not even the novels of Anthony Hope had quite prepared the civilised world for so typical a piece of Balkan savagery as this, and Great Britain led the way in refusing diplomatic recognition to the dynasty restored by such insufferable brutality. Later, of course, Serbia became an ally, due only to the fact that Austria-Hungry had declared war on her, and gradually the world came to remember only Serbia's gallantry and suffering, and to forget her abysmal brutishness.

Yet an indictment of that act of "political expediency", as the authors have somewhere heard it described, was prepared by the mother of the murdered king, and disseminated over the world by a piece of subtlety as typically Balkan in its fashion as the heartlessness that it was intended to condemn. That indictment may be found to-day in thousands of stamp albums: and it will be there when even Marshal Tito is dust.

At the time of the *coup d'état* a new series of postage stamps was in readiness for issue: the series bearing, naturally, the portrait of the dead king. The conspirators, having caused these to be overprinted with an obscuring coat of arms, then commissioned M. Eugène Mouchon, a distinguished French engraver, who had been responsible for the famous French "Droits de l'Homme" design of 1900, to prepare designs for some new stamps to commemorate the coronation of the new king, Peter I.

The design finally accepted consisted of a plaque, showing the twin profiles of King Peter and his ancestor, "Black George", the founder of the Karageorgevitch dynasty. When, however, the stamp had been distributed in its millions of copies, it was found that the profile of the murdered king, Alexander, had been skilfully introduced between the profiles of Peter and Black George, though inverted in relation to theirs (Pl. IV). Although Monsieur Mouchon indignantly denied any hand in this extraordinary stratagem to make the murderers the publicists of their own indictment, the "death mask" is too clear for it ever to have introduced itself into the design by mere chance. In spite of Monsieur Mouchon's denials of complicity in this thoroughly Ruritanian piece of court intrigue, we may perhaps, without offence, decline to accept the distinguished engraver's denials. For one thing, the stamp—a most elegant affair—bears every mark of his own professional skill, and not a sign that anyone else, however competent, "touched it up" after it had left Monsieur Mouchon's hands. For another, it is the sort of plot to which an upright, sensitive, pre-eminently civilised artist would have been expected to lend himself: for the butchering of the Serbian royal family was a bloody deed which shocked a world less inured to such animalism than, alas, is our own! In our opinion, Monsieur Mouchon would not have accepted the commission to design a stamp for King Peter I had he not already been approached by Queen Natalie: that he designed the stamp at all is, in our opinion, the best proof that the famous "Death Mask" was no strange accident, but a calcu-lated act of reproof for a horrible crime.

*   *   *

A face which once appeared on a stamp had less significance, from the point of view of the man who caused it to be there, but was the cause of possibly more fuss than the "death mask" of King Alexander.

In the year before the Canadian currency was changed from the pounds, shillings and pence system to the decimal system based on the dollar, the Honble. Charles Connell was Postmaster-General of New Brunswick, with Cabinet rank and a salary of £600 a year. At that time the Confederation of Canada had not yet taken place, and each of the Canadian provinces issued its own stamps.

The change in currency naturally entailed a change in the denomination of New Brunswick's coins, paper-money and postage stamps, the responsibility for the last falling, of course, to the Postmaster-General.

The original—1851—issue of the province had been designed and printed by the London firm of Perkins, Bacon & Co., but Connell, looking about for a firm who would print the stamps more cheaply, entrusted the preparation of the new "cents" issue to the American Banknote Co., of New York. The values were to be of 1, 2, 5, 10 and 12½ cents, but to these were added a 17-cent value, in order to cover the postage from New Brunswick to London, via New York. The contract with the American engravers was drawn up and signed by Connell, who had full discretion to arrange such matters, and to him also had been left the choice of the designs that the new stamps were to bear.

The stamps, in sheets of one hundred copies, were delivered in April 1860, to the Post Office Department at Fredericton, and, as a matter of course, were examined by the postal officials. It is not hard to imagine the astonishment of the officials when they saw that, while Queen Victoria's head had been used to ornament the 10-cent, and that of the Prince of

Wales the 17-cent, no less a person than the Honble. Charles
Connell himself had been chosen to adorn, with his rugged
empire-builder's features, the 5-cent stamp (Pl. IV) the most
commonly used of all.

Connell, when the stamps were delivered at the provincial
capital, was at home at Woodstock, sixty miles away. The
stamps were due to be put on general sale a day or two later,
so that his astonishment and chagrin were extreme when he
received a telegram from the Provincial Secretary: "Just
received notice from the Governor that new decimal stamps
cannot be issued until approved by Governor in Council.
Have seen Hale. Telegraph him. He can put all right." (Hale
was the Secretary to the Post Office.)

Unfortunately for the Postmaster-General, Hale could not
"put all right", and the stamps were not issued until after
the Provincial Council had met. At the meeting, it was
decided to issue all those stamps which did not bear Connell's
portrait, and that a new 5-cent stamp should be designed,
"bearing the likeness of the Queen". A week after the meeting
had been held, Connell tendered his resignation to the
Governor. It was accepted.

Now there is something most mysterious in this matter of
the "Connell". There is no mystery in human vanity, but
there may be—and there is here—in human folly. For though
all the stamps of the proposed new series did not bear royal
portraits—the 1-cent bore the drawing of a railway engine,
and the 12½-cent, a steamship—Connell must have known
that his action in putting his face on a stamp whose com-
panions bore the likenesses of the Queen and of the Prince
of Wales would not go without the most adverse comment.
Why did he do it?

One explanation is that he gave no order to prepare such
a stamp as the "Connell", but that the Postmaster-General's
face appeared on the 5-cent only because, when the 17-cent
stamp was added to the original series, the American Banknote Company, who had been provided only with five designs,
found themselves one short, and having a portrait of Connell
handy, put this upon the 5-cent stamp on their own authority.

It must be confessed that the story hardly sounds plausible, and that Connell did it to please his daughter sounds little more likely.

There must be an explanation, and doubtless the true one is less—far less—fantastic than those adduced by Connell's political enemies, some of whom drew so far upon their imagination as to suggest that the Postmaster-General, suffering from *folie de grandeur*, intended to revolt against the Crown, set up an independent kingdom of New Brunswick, and found a dynasty in his own person! The "Connell" stamp, these enemies added, was the certain proof of this!

Connell had much to suffer, even from those who did not accuse him of plotting high treason. He was made the subject of countless squibs and lampoons, and an amusing "Ballade in Ye Olde Style" has come down to us from the pages of a stamp-collecting magazine which saw in the Postmaster-General's egotism a rich source of unkind humour.

Connell himself, though he denied that his resignation had anything to do with the stamp which bore his head, acquired the stamps—there were half a million of them—at his own expense, and made a bonfire of the sheets in his back garden. A few were saved, and to-day are catalogued at £150, even though they were never officially issued, and are thus, from the philatelic point of view, hardly to be classed among the regular issues. The stamp bearing the Queen's head which was substituted for the "Connell" is, by one of those ironies of fate which give us a hint sometimes to revise our sense of values, catalogued at 2s. 6d. unused and 3s. 6d. used.

*   *   *

The late Lord Baden-Powell was another who allowed his portrait to be put upon a stamp, with consequences which, though not of lasting ill-effect to his career, were unpleasant enough at the time. As commander of the British garrison besieged in Mafeking, Baden-Powell—a psychologist of rare virtue—sought to sustain the morale of the inhabitants by doing everything possible to avoid their acquiring a "siege mentality". With inexhaustible energy, and with that imagination without which energy is useless, Baden-Powell strove to keep the people of Mafeking busy the day-long in sustaining the ordinary life of the beleaguered town. We are concerned here only with the fact that, among the many "ordinary" things of Mafeking life that this fine administrator endeavoured—and contrived—to preserve, was the postal system. At first, stamps of the Cape of Good Hope, the Bechuanaland Protectorate and British Bechuanaland—all overprinted *Mafeking Besieged*—were used to frank the letters which were, in many ingenious ways, taken out of the town through the Boer patrols.

When the stock of stamps came to an end, Baden-Powell commissioned a local artist and printer to prepare some more. They appeared in two values, 1d. and 3d.: the lower value bearing a not unskilfully executed cut of Sergeant-Major Goodyear (who "managed" the local post) on his bicycle; the higher, the really well-drawn bust of Baden-Powell.

Now the designs of these two stamps deserve some attention. On the "Goodyear" design there is an ornamental scroll above the Sergeant-Major's picture, which bears the legend, SIEGE OF—V.R.—MAFEKING, a crown being drawn above the "V.R.". Underneath the figure of the cycling N.C.O. is written LOCAL POST, and beneath that again, ONE PENNY. The penny stamp, it is hardly necessary to point out, was intended for the franking only of local letters.

The 3d. stamp, on the other hand, has a label above the bust of the then Colonel Baden-Powell which bears only the words, MAFEKING 1900 SIEGE, without the letters "V.R.", and with no crown above. Beneath the bust is the inscription POSTAGE THREEPENCE.

All Britain went mad on the night when, in posters printed in red, black and blue, the news *Mafeking Relieved!* was carried through the streets of London by the yelling newsboys. That frenzied act of homage to a brave man added a new word to the English language: but the "mafficking" of the crowds found no response in the old Queen's heart. When Baden-Powell returned to England, his Sovereign declined to receive him, and but for the accession of a monarch of more liberal views a year later, the career of Baden-Powell might not have been the splendid triumph that it was. For the true measure of that triumph it may be of interest to philatelists to look through their catalogues, and there count the number of stamps which—including those of Russia, Germany and Hungary—have made allusion to the great Scout movement that the defender of Mafeking founded.

*   *   *

There is a story connected with the stamps issued to commemorate the sixtieth birthday of the Dowager Empress of China, in 1894 (Pl. XXI), which, though of high dramatic interest and of considerable currency, is purely apocryphal. We shall retell it here, though, in order to show that the myth-making influences have already begun to work upon the complex of philatelic history, so that the philatelic historian may be warned that his "facts" are no less liable to distortion or fabrication than the facts of other sciences.

The hero of this apocryphal tale is a Monsieur R. A. de Villard, a French *artiste-peintre* and engraver of repute, who held a senior position in the Chinese Imperial Customs. To him came the commission to prepare the designs for the commemorative postage stamps, and—so the legend goes— "through an unwitting breach of the rigid etiquette of the Chinese court, this commission cost the unfortunate artist his life."

We suspect that the then unpopularity of the Chinese provided the essential credibility of the tale: for the story of M. de Villard's stamps gained currency around the time of the Boxer Rising, and to a generation which had accepted the late Guy Boothby's *Doctor Nikola* as a best-seller, almost anything unpleasant concerning the "heathen Chinee" was credible.

In the legend, M. de Villard submitted his designs, in which he had abbreviated the inscription "Imperial Chinese Post" to "Imp. Chin. Post", only to incur the severest censure since any abbreviation of an official title was in direct contravention of Chinese manners and customs. "More heinous

still, in the eyes of Chinese officialdom, was the employment
of the Imperial purple in the colour scheme, the use of this
colour being strictly forbidden, except to members of the
Imperial Court."

For a time the fate of the hapless artist trembled in the
balance, and it was a question whether or not he should be
beheaded for his unconscious insult to the throne. At length
he was despatched on a forlorn surveying expedition to the
heart of Thibet, whence he never returned.

M. Villard recognised that such a journey amounted practically to a sentence of death, and writing on his departure
to a friend in England, informed him that in all probability
it would be the last letter he would receive from him: a
prophecy that unfortunately proved only too true. So ran the
story.

In fact, M. de Villard retired on pension—his retirement
being quite unconnected with any abbreviation of the
Imperial titles or unauthorised use of the Imperial tincture—
and lived peacefully to an advanced age.

*   *   *

The famous "Post Office" stamps of Mauritius were engraved by a watchmaker and jeweller named Barnard, of Port
Louis, the island's capital, who charged £10 for engraving
the plate—for two stamps: 1d. and 2d.—and 10s. per
thousand stamps, printing charge.

The issue of postage stamps for Mauritius had been authorised by the Governor, Sir William Gomm, and it was desired
to have a first issue ready in order to frank the invitations to
a fancy-dress ball that Lady Gomm was to give at Government
House on September 30th, 1847.

Reference has been made elsewhere to the rarity and the
value of the "Post Office Mauritius" stamps: here we are
concerned only with the production of the originals.

Barnard, on having his estimate accepted by the island's
Postmaster, J. Stuart Brownrigg, looked around for a piece of
copper suitable to take the necessary engravings. He found
one about the size of an ordinary lady's visiting-card, which

had been used for printing-off the trade-cards of a Port Louis hotel. On the back of this copper plate Barnard engraved— crudely enough, in all conscience—the two designs for which the Government of Mauritius had paid the watchmaker £10, and of which the printed copies were to fetch anything up to £5,000.

Major E. B. Evans, an early philatelic historian, during a tour of duty in Mauritius, set out to investigate the origins of the "Post Office" issue, and to acquire, if possible, a specimen for himself. In both these intentions he succeeded: he discovered the original of the estimate that Barnard had submitted to the Postmaster (which estimate is now in the Tapling Collection at the British Museum) and he bought the collection of a local resident, Mr. Buger, for Fcs. 250— say £10. This collection contained a fine specimen of the 1d. "Post Office" on its original envelope.

Major Evans was in Mauritius in 1878: it was thirty-four years later, on a hot summer's day on 1912, that a friend of the late Mr. Nevile Stocken, a well-known stamp dealer, and the man whom Mr. Bonar called in to sell what was afterwards known as the "King's Copy" of the unused 2d. "Post Office" (No. XXIV), walked into the dealer's office, and shook that gentleman out of a summer somnolence with the startling question: "What would you say if I could show you the plate of the 'Post Office Mauritius'?"

Suspecting a joke, Mr. Stocken answered his friend with discourteous abruptness, but the friend had not been joking. He told Mr. Stocken to take his hat and stick, and to walk around the corner, where he would have the pleasure of bringing the dealer face to face with the owner of the plate.

The owner of this unique philatelic treasure was a Colonel Colnaghi, a grandson of Lady Gomm, who had found it while going through some family papers which had been stored in the strong-rooms of Drummond's Bank, Charing Cross. Sir William Gomm, whose correspondence with the Colonial Office—preserved in the Public Records Office, Chancery Lane *—shows him to have taken the keenest interest in the

* See "*Post Office Mauritius*" 1847, by Michael Harrison, for a full account of this historic issue (Stamp Collecting, London).

stamp issue of the Mauritius, had kept the copper plate as a souvenir, and it had lain among Sir William's papers since his death in 1875.

Colonel Colnaghi had had no idea that this small piece of engraved metal had any value, philatelic or otherwise, when he came across it in looking through the Gomm papers; but a casual mention of the plate to a friend brought about his meeting with Mr. Stocken, and the dealer's purchase of something which, in less scrupulous hands, might well have upset the market in "Post Office Mauritius".

The news of the plate's discovery certainly thrilled the world of Philately, and the non-philatelic world, too, began to be interested in the discovery when the Colonial Office did not hesitate to threaten Mr. Stocken with everything short of *la peine forte et dure* when he refused to surrender the plate to "its rightful owners". Mr. Stocken pointed out that he had entered into a perfectly normal financial transaction; that he had been offered something at a certain price; that the price had been paid; and that he was now in lawful possession of the object bought.

After a decidedly acrimonious correspondence, the Colonial Office gave up what all who knew Mr. Stocken will realise was, from the very beginning, a most unequal contest, and a few months later the plate (Pl. XXIV) came into the possession of Mr. Sidney Loder, a well-known collector. Later Mr. Loder sold it to the French collector M. Maurice Burrus.

*　　　*　　　*

One of the first of those who helped to raise, by their care and integrity, the schoolboy's hobby of "stamp collecting" to that of Philately which, before the jubilee of the postage stamp, was to include some of the world's most famous names among its lovers, was the Belgian dealer J. B. Moens, an early dealer, and the publisher of *Le Timbre Poste*.

Unfortunately, the standards that Moens was attempting to establish for the guidance of the new philatelic trade were not by any means of the sort which would appeal to those of his rivals who could see in stamps only a means of fleecing the credulous young and the ignorant adult. While such people as Moens were attempting to impose a high professional standard upon the stamp trade, there were others whose professional standards were those of the catch-penny at a Saturday market.

One of the worst offenders against the system of commercial probity that Moens was endeavouring to introduce into the conduct of philatelic affairs was a Parisian stamp dealer and publisher, Monsieur A. Maury, proprietor of *Le Timbrophile*, whose many irregularities included the pirating of the articles that Moens gave much research to preparing. Angered by the flagrant and impudent "lifting" of his articles by his Parisian rival—this all took place before the days of the international agreements on copyright—Moens resolved to make Maury the victim of his own dishonesty.

Now, just as the Treaty of Paris, which brought the Crimean War to an end, overlooked the town of Berwick-on-Tweed (which had declared war against Russia), so the Treaty of Vienna, which concluded the Napoleonic Wars, left the territory of Moresnet, which lies on the Belgo-German frontier, with an unsettled status. By agreement between Belgium and Germany, the district was administered jointly by the two countries, the district itself being accorded a nominal independence, though neither coins nor postage stamps for Moresnet had ever been issued. In fact, the status of Moresnet after the Napoleonic Wars closely resembled that of the New Hebrides Condominium.

A letter was printed in the April 1867 issue of *Le Timbre Poste*, dated April 1st, and signed J. S. Neom, giving details of an alleged stamp issue for Moresnet. To a full description of the design of the new stamps was added a note that the preparation of the issue had been undertaken by the firm of De Visch et Lirva, of Brussels.

Monsieur Maury fell into the trap that his oft-victimised rival had set for him: not only did the unscrupulous Parisian print the details of the Moresnet issue as given by Moens' "correspondent", but—in his capacity as dealer—offered to supply the stamps listed in the article that he had pirated.

It is a pity that there were no *Sunday Times* crosswords in those days to sharpen up Monsieur Maury's wits, and to spare him the regret that his falling into so simple a trap must have caused. For, in the following number of *Le Timbre Poste*, Moens pointed out that "J. S. Neom" was simply an anagram of J. Moens; that "Visch" was the Flemish for fish (French: *poisson*), and "Lirva" the French word "Avril" (April) reversed; and the whole name of the imaginary firm of De Visch et Lirva nothing more than the French phrase for "April Fool"—*Poisson d'Avril*: a fact that the highly suspicious date on the "J. S. Neom" letter might have caused Maury to suspect.

There were, of course, no stamps of Moresnet; there never had been—and Maury had offered to supply them. One wonders what would have happened had Moens kept the revelation of his jest back a little longer, and had sent a money-order to his Parisian rival for a complete set of the new issues!

*　　　*　　　*

Very many people collect stamps, though not all for philatelic purposes. In an earlier chapter we have told the story of the Italian artist who used the valuable "Trinacria" issues of Naples for the purpose of decorating a table-top, and the authors quite recently stopped to look in at the window of an antique shop in Soho, in which a tea-tray was exposed for sale. The tray had a glass bottom, and beneath the glass a most decorative panel, composed entirely of stamps, arranged in a geometric pattern. Judging by the date of the stamps used, and the general design of the tray, we estimated the period of the piece as *circa* 1880. But, alas and alack, there were no valuable stamps among the hundreds which had been used to make up the panel.

We have also seen a most patriotic portrait of Her Late Majesty Queen Victoria, executed by some patiently fervent imperialist entirely in postage stamps, and a fine folding screen covered from top to bottom with a chequer-design composed of alternate penny and halfpenny Great Britain King Edwards.

But the prize for this sort of decoration must surely go to the reverend gentleman who is the subject of the following paragraph, quoted from *The Philatelic Magazine*, of August 9th, 1924:

"Perhaps the most patiently papered house in America is that of the Rev. A. Bucci, a retired priest, who has papered two rooms of his home here (Burbank, Cal.) with 149,242 postage stamps.

"It took Father Bucci more than thirty years to collect the stamps, and practically every nation in the world is represented in the geometrical designs of the wall-borders and in the colour schemes employed on walls and ceilings.

"On one of the ceilings is a design of the Stars and Stripes, with Italian stamps forming the blue field, and American two-cent stamps supplying the red stripes.

"The brown staff holding the banner consists of Canadian stamps, while the white stripes of the flag are formed by the strips of bare ceiling remaining after Father Bucci completed his paper-hanging."

It is fitting that a nation which has always had a tender regard for the Biggest Ever should be able to show Father Bucci's fine example of grandiose patience, but Britain can show examples relatively astonishing: Mr. Jones, Vicar of Llandinam, writing in the same issue of *The Philatelic Magazine*, tells us that he has "a room which is papered with stamps in an effective and bright design . . . down to the skirting board", and an editorial note records the existence of a room at the Rising Sun, North Bersted, near Bognor Regis, which is papered with 76,795 stamps—just over half the number used for Father Bucci's artistic effort!

Mention of Father Bucci's stamp-papered room in Burbank reminds us of the advertisements which still appear regularly in religious newspapers and journals, asking sympathisers to collect postage stamps "for Missions". We have often wondered what financial benefit the missionary societies got from the receipt of these stamps: for even the commonest—indeed, particularly the commonest—were asked for; and we remember to have been in a City office when two Sisters of Mercy called to collect the stamps torn, for their use, from the firm's correspondence. Common politeness forbade us to enquire of the religious ladies for what purpose they collected this (philatelically considered) almost worthless material; but an advertisement in a recent copy of an American stamp magazine provided us with a clue. Under the heading, "Clearance of Surplus Stock of Mixtures" all sold at so much per pound weight, are such items as "United States Common Mixture" and "Finland Finest Quality Mixture"—which has a certain tobaccoish flavour about it. And listed at $2.85 per lb. is "Denmark Government and Convent Mixture": so part of the mystery is solved—not all, for we still do not know who buys the "mixtures".

*   *   *

As our subject has come around to missionaries, we may end this chapter by recalling one of the few stamp issues that has been produced on a typewriter. For it was a missionary, the Rev. Ernest Millar, C.M.S., who prepared them at the request of Mr. G. Wilson, then Deputy Commissioner of Uganda.

A British Protectorate over Uganda had been declared in 1894, and in the early part of the following year Mr. Wilson decided to investigate the possibilities of a local post. He talked the matter over with Mr. Millar—the owner of the only typewriter in the whole Protectorate—and the two men agreed that, since the need for a postal service was most urgent, they should organise one: Mr. Millar to prepare the necessary postage stamps on his typewriter.

The record of Mr. Millar's agreement to print a "sheet of all values, from 10 to 50 shells", is entered in the missionary's diary, under date of March 4th, 1895, and two days later an official notice gave the details of the proposed postal service. That the stamps typewritten by Mr. Millar on March 14th were genuine is evident from the final paragraph of the official notice, which states that letters insufficiently stamped would not be posted.

The 2½-cents black-and-orange Surinam, 1892, the Fiji Times "Express", and British Guiana stamps of 1850 have all designs whose simplicity borders upon (and, in some opinions, oversteps) the limits of the barbarous; but there was surely never a stamp so lacking in all that finish that we associate with official documents as the stamps that Mr. Millar typed on his machine.

The "design" consisted merely of the letters "U.G." (for Uganda Government), with the denomination—in numerals —in the centre of the stamp, the absence of a printer's rule being compensated for by the not unadroit employment of the hyphen and apostrophe on Mr. Millar's typewriter. But the missionary was no expert typist: there are plenty of errors, of the sort that one associates with a limited comprehension of the peculiarities of a typewriter (Pl. IV).

Several "printings" were made, and in the month after the first stamps had been run off, Mr. Millar received a new typewriter from England, whose type-face was different from that of his old machine. It is easy, then, to date the "Uganda Cowries", as they are called. At the end of 1895 Mr. Millar substituted a violet for a black ribbon, so that here again is a means by which these odd but fiscally genuine stamps may be dated. Properly printed stamps of Uganda came into use in November 1896, and with their coming Mr. Millar's typewritten issue ceased. Some years ago the original typewriter, a "Barlock", was on view at a London Stamp exhibition. To-day some of these primitive stamps are valued by collectors at up to £20 apiece.

CHAPTER XII

Design and the Stamp

STAMP-DESIGN is a subject which has received far less than the attention that it has merited; and the wide currency of some "infallible" beliefs with regard to the early issues has prevented a clearly objective analysis of design in itself, as differentiated from the purpose of the design. Preconceived opinion, in philatelic science as elsewhere, has too long been the almost insurmountable obstacle to a just estimate of the success and failure of those artists responsible for the multifarious designs of the world's stamps.

For instance, it has long been an article of faith among philatelists that there has never been a stamp to equal the first stamp of all: the deservedly famous "Penny Black". To quote an authority, "it is the embodiment of all that a postage stamp should be, combining artistry with utility, and dignity with simplicity."

Now, this is true enough, provided that we consider the "Penny Black" as, not only the first stamp ever to have been issued, but (and this is important) as the only stamp which was ever destined to be issued. For as soon as even one other country began to issue postage stamps, an inherent fault in the design of the "Penny Black" became apparent, though that fault was concealed so long as the "Penny Black" remained the only postage stamp in the world.

The fault was this: the design gave no indication of the country of origin, and the indisputable claim that the design, as it stood, was instantly recognisable, anywhere in the world, still does not alter the fact that the design was inherently faulty, since it did not provide against a failure, on the part of some foreign postal official, to recognise the source of the stamp's origin.

It may be argued, of course, that until the introduction of

universal language the incorporation of the name of the
issuing country in the stamp-design may be of as little assistance to a postal official of another country as no name at all;
and, in fact, it would seem that the "recognition-index"
must necessarily rely, until the introduction or adoption of
a universal language—or universally understood language—
on the art-work of a stamp, rather than on the intrinsic
meaning of its legend.

During the latter part of the last century an attempt was
made to make the legends on stamps universally comprehen-
sible by adopting the French language: in those days not
only the language of diplomacy but also the language of
"polite intercourse" all over the world. Especially did the
governments of those countries whose language was written
with a non-Latin script employ French on their stamps, as
Persia, Afghanistan, Egypt and Ethiopia still do; but the
growth of nationalism during recent years has tended to make
it a matter of national pride that the design of stamps shall
not appear to be influenced by the needs of any other country
but that responsible for the stamps' issue.

In another chapter the *purpose* of the various stamp-designs
has been considered: here we shall examine the design, considered independently of any propagandist purpose or use.

First of all, what basic conditions does any perfectly designed
stamp need to satisfy? If we list these conditions, we shall be
better able to estimate the success so far achieved in stamp-
design; and we shall find these conditions by asking what
functions any stamp needs to discharge.

A stamp is a receipt for prepaid postage. The amount of
money paid for postal service should, therefore, be clearly
shown, no matter that, by international agreement, certain
postal values are also denoted by the colours used. The first
function of a stamp, then, is to show clearly its monetary
value, since the monetary value governs the limits of a stamp's
franking-power.

Only second in importance to a stamp's clear indication of
its value comes the clear indication of its country of origin:
and this comes second because, within the country of origin,

PLATE XXI

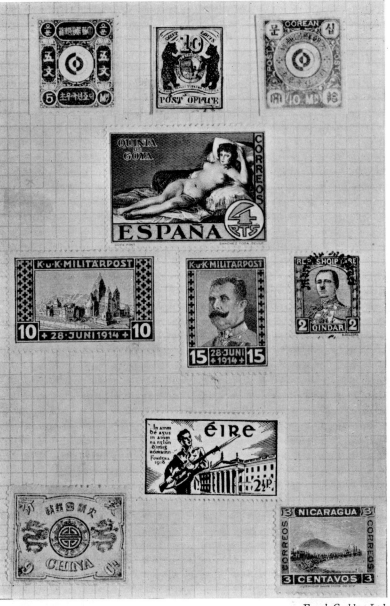

Frank Godden Ltd.

First stamps of Korea; "St. Louis Bears"; stamp that shocked America;
relics of the Sarajevo tragedy; from President to King of Albania; "Easter
Week" commemoration in Eire; Chinese "Jubilee" stamp, 1894; stamp
that influenced the Panama Canal

PLATE XXII

SOVIET STAMP DESIGNS

"Cutting the fetters"; "The Triumph of the Revolution"; Marshal Suvarov; Order of the Great Patriotic War; Karl Marx's grave at Highgate; Meyerhold Theatre, Moscow; ice-breaker *Josef Stalin*; flags of the War Allies

the purchasers of the stamps will not need to know whence
the stamp originates. It is necessary only for the postal officials
of other lands to know where stamps originate.

It is *not* a function of the design either to incorporate some
seal of authority which is the jealously guarded prerogative
of the state or to incorporate in the design some forger-
baffling tricks. The designer should not be called upon to
outwit the forger: that duty belongs to the engraver and
printer.

Contrary to generally accepted theory, the *size* of the stamp
as well as its *shape* is the concern of the designer, for one of
the basic conditions that a well-designed stamp—any stamp,
for that matter—needs to satisfy is that it shall be convenient
to handle; not too large for the average envelope, and not too
small to be a nuisance both to stick on and to see. Like the
soap advertised in a modern series of newspaper announcements, a stamp should be "not too little, not too much".

And, since the area to be covered by the designer must—
or should, at any rate—affect profoundly the design, the size
of the stamp is certainly his concern; just as the shape is his
concern, since shape may provide one of those elements of
"recognisability" by which a stamp's origin is instantly
apparent.

The use of a triangular shape for the first (1853) issue of
the Cape of Good Hope has often been criticised adversely,
mostly on the grounds that the choice of the triangular shape
indicated a capriciousness of taste unworthy of a government.
But the choice, in fact, had much to recommend it. Unprece-
dented at the time of issue, the unusual shape was sufficient
in itself to indicate the origin of the stamp, and did not need
either the sitting allegorical figure of Hope or the lettering
which ran around the border.

Since then, the triangular shape has been adopted by
other governments—among them Liberia, Latvia, Salvador,
Bohemia-and-Moravia, Bolivia, Paraguay, Nicaragua (which
also issued a lozenge-shaped stamp to celebrate the centenary
of the foundation of Managua, in 1847), Newfoundland,
Netherlands Indies and several French colonies—and the

value of the triangular shape as a "recognition-index" in itself has, of course, been lost with the multiplication of triangular stamps.

Since the international agreements following the establishment of the Universal Postal Union in 1874 have called for the common use of certain colours to denote values—thus, originally, the colour green indicated 1 halfpenny or 5 centimes French or 5 centimos Spanish, etc., while red denoted one penny or 2 cents American or 10 centimes French, and so on—the indication of the country of origin by colour alone presents certain difficulties.

With the passing of time, and frequent fluctuations in international rates of exchange, the standard "Postal Union" colours (so-called) no longer indicate a particular monetary value, but rather a particular rate of postage. The existing British 2½d. stamp, for example, is printed in red to indicate that it is intended primarily for internal (and to some extent inter-Commonwealth) postage, the 1½d. denomination is green because it is chiefly used for printed matter; whilst the 4d. blue represents the charge levied by H.M. Postmaster-General upon 1-oz. letters addressed to places outside the Commonwealth but within the Universal Postal Union. The idea is the same; only its application has changed.

It has been suggested that a certain way of making all stamps instantly recognisable would be to mark each with the national flag; but this would not allow for the changes in colour corresponding to changes in value, and to keep one colour while altering the monetary values marked on the stamps would be to put a greatly added burden on the postal-clerks, who have come to rely upon colour as an aid to the recognition, not only of the source of the stamps, but also of their values. A recommendation adopted by the Rome Convention of the Universal Postal Union, in 1906, that the postal values of stamps should be boldly shown in Arabic numerals, as well as, or instead of, in words, has, regrettably, been more honoured in breach than observance.

Symbols, too, are useful as aids to recognition so long as nations may "copyright" them by international agreement:

but they lose their value when they are employed by more than one state. Thus, from 1919 to 1924 the ancient symbol of the "lictoral fasces" appeared on the stamps of Poland, as it appeared on a Swiss issue of 1911, and again (in the arms of the Canton of St. Gall) on an issue of 1924. The lictoral fasces is also to be found—as part of the coat of arms of the French Republic—on the 1911 stamps of New Hebrides and all succeeding issues up to 1949. But with the adoption by Mussolini of this ancient symbol as the badge of his "new order" the symbol was dropped from the Polish designs, as from the Swiss and, eventually, from those of New Hebrides.

Again, there is something peculiarly confusing about the use by one nation of symbols associated with other nations. To anyone but a philatelist such an issue as, for instance, that of Soviet Russia for 1943, to commemorate the Teheran Three Power Conference and the 26th anniversary of the October Revolution must seem anything but specifically Russian. This design shows a memorial tablet, flanked with the flags of Soviet Russia, Great Britain and the United States, all three flags being shown as of equal size, with that of the United States in the foreground (Pl. XXII).

And the same objection applies with even more force to the design issued on June 14th, 1944—"United Nations' Day". Here the same three flags are set within an oval frame, the flags of Great Britain and the United States being especially bold, while the initials "C.C.C.P." (U.S.S.R.) are engraved in the very smallest size.

Leaving aside altogether any question of artistic merit, the ideal stamp-design is one which indicates, as clearly as possible, the country of origin and the value, so that, in a highly technical sense, such stamps as, say, the half-groschen of Hanover, 1860, the 2c., 5c., and 13c. of Hawaii, 1851 (among the most valuable stamps in the world, by the way), and the 1c. of Spain, 1933 (one of the very plainest designs ever issued) are superior to the most artistic products of the stamp-designer's skill. The last-mentioned stamp, for instance, consists only of a crown on a plain background, with the word "España" (Spain) below; the figure "1" very bold in the centre of the stamp, with the word "centimo" in the lower edge of the frame, the numeral being flanked on each side with the word "Correos" (Posts). Nothing, in fact, could be plainer, more starkly utilitarian, than this postal label; but its very starkness emphasises the vast distance that stamp-designers have come from the basic in their search for novelty.

For this plain Spanish stamp has everything that a postage stamp needs. It is small enough to be handled easily, and yet large enough to carry its message plainly. It has, clearly marked, the name of the country of origin, the value of the postage paid, and the Spanish word for "posts", to indicate the label's purpose and function.

Only by the substitution of an international language for the Spanish used on the stamp could this design be improved.

Yet, in spite of its utilitarian perfection, the class to which this stamp belongs is one of the smallest in the whole field of Philately.

*   *   *

The reason is not hard to seek. Governments are concerned, in issuing new stamps, with something more than a plain statement of the stamps' origin and the amount of money paid for each specimen.

Although it has, in fact, nothing to do with the efficiency of the stamp to frank a letter, there is a question of that imponderable but highly important concept of "sovereignty" to be considered in preparing the design: and it is the presence of this concept in the mind of those who order and those who design stamps which has been responsible for the great way that stamps have come from the plainness which is all that pure utility demands.

When the wise Solomon said that there was nothing new under the sun, he was calling our attention to the fact that there is no innovation which does not owe much to the circumstances in which it is born; which does not bear within itself the strongest memory of what it has replaced.

There is a point in connection with stamp-design to be borne in mind. Like all other inventions, the postage stamp did not begin in a state of primitive simplicity; but rather as an adaptation of something else. Just as the first railway-train was an adaptation of and an improvement upon the stage-coach, and the first motor-car an adaptation of and an improvement upon the horse-drawn carriage, so the first stamp of all —the famous "Penny Black"— was profoundly influenced, not less in sentiment than in design, by something which had gone before. In the case of the stamp, the preceding influence was the coin; and, in fact, as one of the authors has pointed out elsewhere, the problem of designing the prototype stamp was "solved, literally, by squaring the circle. In other words, the head of the sovereign that, from time immemorial, had adorned the circular coins of the realm was transferred to a rectangle of paper 'just large enough to bear the stamp, and covered at the back with a glutinous wash'."

The first stamp, then, was not really designed as a stamp: it was, in effect, no more than a paper coin, on the preparation of which was lavished all the engravers' skill commonly used in preparing a banknote. Indeed, it was not until several decades had passed since the introduction of the postage stamp that designers began to consider stamp-design on its own merits, and not subtly influenced by the tradition of coin-design.

*   *   *

Now, just as most coinage since the days of the Roman Empire has borne either the effigy of the ruler of the state or some allegorical figure or emblem symbolising the state, so the first stamp continued the ancient tradition by bearing the formalised head of the Sovereign; and those governments which adopted the postage stamp within the decade or so after 1840 adhered to the pattern already set by Great Britain. The 1849 issue of Belgium, the 1847 issue of the United States of America, the 1852 issue of Holland and the 1859 issue of Hanover all follow the British lead in design; and, as we shall see, the pattern set by the original British issue still exerts considerable influence in stamp-design, even in face of the strong competition from other artistic influences (Pl. XXIII).

Some coins, instead of bearing the ruler's head—either as a portrait-bust or a mere conventionalised effigy—carry the arms of the state or some badge or symbol identified with it.

In the same way, where the first stamp issues did not bear the ruler's head, they bore a coat of arms or a badge; and into this second class come the first stamps of the Papal States (1852), Parma (1852), Brunswick (1852) and Mecklenburg-Strelitz (1864). This class, again, established a tradition which is still strong in influence over contemporary design.

The third class of prototype-stamps is that which shows the least influence of the coin-tradition, and derives more from already existing fiscal labels. Into this third class come the "Bull's Eye" Brazil issue of 1843 (which has merely the value in numerals, on an engine-turned background, and nothing else), the Hyderabad issue of 1869, the Danish issue of 1851, the 2-ore to 6-ore values in the Swedish issue of 1872, and the famous "Lady McLeod", of 1847. This class, too, has produced many modern examples.

*   *   *

To these three "prototype" classes—two derived from the tradition of the coin, and one derived from the tradition of the fiscal label or government "stamp"—the nineties of the last century saw the addition of a fourth, and most important, class: the "pictorial".

Like so many other innovations which have had a world-wide influence, the "pictorial" stamp originated within the British Empire; appearing, in 1894, as an issue of the British North Borneo (Chartered) Company.

Naturally, the pictorial stamp had a history behind it, and it would be possible to make out a case for an earlier appearance of the "pictorial". The 3d. Canada, 1851, showing a beaver, could be regarded as a "pictorial"; and there is no doubt that the various Columbus commemoratives of 1892 broke away from the old tradition of the ruler's head or the state's emblem or the post-office receipt.

They were truly pictorial; and yet, in a manner which is better understood by observing the North Borneo stamps of 1894 than in listening to any explanation, the "pictorial" stamp, which is so much a feature of present-day philatelic

art, did not enter the field of Philately until the British North
Borneo Company issued its series showing a Dyak chief, a
"Roussa" (or Malay stag), a sago palm, a pheasant, a dhow,
a crocodile and a fine view of Mt. Kinabalu.

Perhaps here it would be as well to point out that the North
Borneo issue must rank as the original "pictorials", and that
the U.S. issue of 1861—even though this showed a post-rider,
a locomotive, the S.S. *Adriatic*, the landing of Columbus and
the signing of the Declaration of Independence—cannot have
that honour, because of the convention which holds that
originality is not so much first appearance alone as that
appearance which influences a fashion. A certain Mr. Hugh
Mackintosh patented a pneumatic tyre in 1848, forty years
before Dr. Dunlop again patented a pneumatic tyre; but it
is Dr. Dunlop who—rightly—is regarded as the inventor of
the pneumatic tyre, for it was he who introduced that
wonderful invention to the use of mankind.

Just so, though the government of the United States issued
a set of true pictorials in 1869, the new fashion did not "take
on" until the North Borneo Company issued its set in 1894;
the reason why the second issue had an appeal that the first
lacked being doubtless attributable to the fact that the U.S.
1869 stamps are most conservatively engraved, the scenes
being contained within ornamental frames which take up as
much space as the scenes themselves, while with the North
Borneo issue (Pl. XIII) the frames are not only subordinated
to the pictures that they enclose, but are printed in a different
colour. There was certainly an eye-catching appeal about the
North Borneo issue which was missing in the earlier U.S.
issue.

The "pictorial" stamp had an immediate and world-wide
success—especially among those governments who looked to
their issues of postage stamps to produce some much-needed
revenue. The rocky finances of certain Central and South
American states were the healthier for some really splendid
"pictorials", with which the writers remember to have filled
page after page of their Stanley Gibbons albums as boys; but
governments with more stable currencies did not despise the

new fashion, and the United States, after having dropped "pictorials" (excluding the Columbus commemorative of 1893) for nearly thirty years, readopted them as a permanent feature of its postal issues. So much so, that a complete study of the development of the "pictorial", from the heavy-framed "Lake Steamer" of the Pan-American Exhibition issue of 1901 to the 1944 stamp showing the S.S. *Savannah* crossing the Atlantic, may be made in observing the changes which have come over the American "pictorials"—though it must be borne in mind that American traditionalism has always gone hand in hand with the well-known American love of novelty, and that, while constantly adopting new techniques of design and printing, the U.S. Postmasters-General have never abandoned established types. Thus, not only is the ½c. 1932 of the "Bicentenary of Washington" issue identical in artistic "feeling" with an issue as old as that of the "Presidents" of 1870, but the 1940 "Novelists" issue is designed in the very spirit of the 1903 2c. red, which shows the head of Washington. This strong sense of the past, which still characterises the taste of the U.S. Post Office, has had the effect of preventing the adoption in America of the most "modern" types of design, types which will be considered shortly.

Other established nations adopted the "pictorial". Britain, though sticking resolutely to the non-pictorial tradition, so far as issues for the home-country were concerned, authorised many "pictorials" for the Colonies; and the French colonial empire was not backward in producing some fine stamp pictures. Austria-Hungary produced, in the issue for the sixtieth anniversary of the Emperor Franz Josef's accession, one excellent stamp, in the 2h., showing the imperial palace of Schönbrunn; but two years earlier, for the protectorate of Bosnia-Herzegovina, the Austro-Hungarian government had issued a truly superb set of "pictorials", the 25h. and 1k. values being sinisterly memorable as showing scenes from ill-starred Sarajevo.

It is possible that there have never, in the history of Philately, been stamps more elegantly designed or better

PLATE XXIII

CONTRASTS IN EARLY STAMP DESIGNS

U.S.A., 1847; Canada, 1851; Chile, 1853; Barbados, 1858; Brazil, 1843;
Ionian Islands, 1859; Van Diemen's Land, 1853; Victoria, 1850; Queens-
land, 1860; New South Wales, 1850; Holland, 1852; Switzerland, Basel,
1845; France, 1849; Sicily, 1859; Roumania, 1858; Tuscany, 1851;
Saxony, 1856

PLATE XXIV

H. R. Harmer Ltd.

Robson Lowe Ltd.

(*Above*)

Famous "Post Office Mauritius" Stamps—and the plate from which they were printed

(*Left*)

Britain's rarest stamp; an enlargement of one of only a dozen copies known to collectors

Four out of forty 1s. British "Olympic Games" stamps discovered with surcharge "1 RUPEE" for use by postal agency at Muscat, *doubly printed*. Valued at £400. Enlarged photograph

executed than these which marked the apotheosis of the
doomed Austro-Hungarian empire.

*　　　　*　　　　*

But there was another artistic influence at work at the end
of the nineteenth century which was, in common with other
artistic influences, to make its mark on stamp-design.

The English artist-craftsman William Morris had taken an
extraordinary interest in lettering, which he felt had sadly
deteriorated both in manuscript and in printing. Turning
back to the mediæval scribes and the Renascence typographers
for inspiration, Morris developed some pleasing "hands" of
his own, which he used in preparing illuminated MSS.—
notably of the "Rubaiyat" of his friend Edward FitzGerald.
Morris also designed new type-founts, and printed some
books, at his own private press, which marked a startling
revival of the printer's art. The influence of Morris extended
far beyond the borders of his own country, and the American
printer Goudy, inspired by Morris's work, produced some
founts of type worthy to be ranked with those of the old
masters of type: with Jenson and Aldus and Garamond and
Plantin and Baskerville and Bodoni and Gill. The last-named
artist was responsible for the admirable lettering and decoration of the British stamps of King George VI's reign.

Perhaps no other single artistic influence has been so
powerful as that wielded by Morris; and his influence was
most clearly seen in the new interest in lettering as an art-
form in itself. Where inscriptions, though well written, had
been regarded as subordinate to the design that they explained,
the letters themselves were now elevated to a position in
which they were regarded as capable of providing a satisfying
design in themselves.

The result of this new approach to lettering is to be seen
in the vogue for covering objects with inscriptions. Not only
jugs and boxes and mirror-frames, but mantelpieces and
wardrobes and even the front-doors of houses were adorned,
at the end of the nineteenth century, with mottoes and tags of
poetry. "They say? What say they? Let them say" was carved

on Bernard Shaw's mantelpiece. "Open locks, Whoever knocks!" is still to be found carved deep into the front-door of a Cheyne Walk house.

What has this to do with stamp-design?

A lot, indeed.

This new approach to lettering, this artistic attempt to raise the dignity of writing to that which had been enjoyed by the "lettera Romana" in the days of Imperial Rome, appealed curiously to the Dutch, a nation which has always had a natural dislike for excessive ornamentation.

It is a tempting thought to relate this Dutch love of—what shall we call it?—"plain-ness"?—with the fact that the Dutch were the first of the Western peoples to become on intimate terms with the Japanese and Chinese; that they contrived to overcome the dislike—the xenophobic hatred—of these Oriental peoples, where other European nations failed. And it may be so: community of taste does often make for community of sentiment, and there remains the fact—explain it how we may—that the Dutch "got on" with the Japanese and the Chinese where no other Europeans could.

Calligraphy is an art greatly honoured and widely practised among the Oriental peoples—and particularly among the Chinese and the Japanese (whose culture was derived originally from the Chinese).

Their artists have, through centuries, given of their genius to raising calligraphy to a position of pre-eminence among their arts; and, with both the Chinese and the Japanese, writing, *in itself*, and in no way associated with other designs, has long been held to receive worthily all the honour that other peoples pay to the graphic arts.

The attempt, by William Morris and his sympathisers, to restore calligraphy to the position of honour that it had enjoyed among the Western peoples some centuries earlier met with an extraordinary response among the Dutch, and, following an undistinguished issue of 1898—the lower values on a design of unrelieved ordinariness, the higher in an uninspired Victorian baroque—the Dutch designers began to put out issues in which the lettering dominates the whole design, so that all accessory ornament begins to lose its pictorial quality and takes on the formalism of the lettering that it supports.

This taste for formalism as opposed to realism in design did not extend to the issues for the Dutch colonies—at least, only partly. The Dutch colonial issues combine the formal (there is a 1936 design for Surinam which has a marked affinity with the "Lady McLeod" of seventy years earlier) with the frankly pictorial, such as the 1945 issue of the same Dutch colony, where the 7½c. shows a sugar-cane train in a style forcibly reminiscent of the U.S. pictorials of 1912.

Obviously, where lettering is held to be the most important part of the design, the "supporting" ornament will tend to be reduced to the minimum, while where there is a pictorial element this will inevitably be formalised so as not to detract from (but rather to lend force to) the legend which is the main element of the design.

A design produced in this spirit must come very near to perfection in stamp-design; and certainly it would be hard to find better designs than some of the "formal" types produced by the Dutch and by other nations inspired by Dutch example.

The 1929 Charity (Child Welfare) issue, for instance, is an almost ideal example of what may be done with formal elements. A highly stylised, yet by no means unnatural, figure of a child riding on a dolphin is placed between (at top) the word *Nederland* and (at bottom) the phrase *Voor het Kind* ("For the Child"), while in the upper left-hand corner is placed the numeral. Nothing could be plainer than this white design on a monochrome background; and nothing could be more effective and more practical.

Indeed, it is the feeling that the formal does truly come nearest to what is ideal in stamp-design which has caused so many other nations—though still inspired by Dutch example —to issue what I had better call the "calligraphic" type of stamp; and one of the most curious results of the world-wide adoption of this class of design is seen in the fact that the Netherlands 1928 Olympic Games issue, especially the values showing the footballer, could have been designed by the same artist responsible, ten years later, for the Lithuania 1938 First National Olympiad Fund issue.

Again, the 5f. value of the 1939 issue of the Principality of Liechtenstein, showing the "decollated" head of Prince Francis Joseph II surrounded by the unframed legend *Fuerstentum—Liechtenstein*—(Principality of Liechtenstein) is *identical* in artistic conception—in what commercial artists call the "lay-out"—with the 30s., 50s., and 1y. values of the 1946 Japan issue, marking the seventy-fifth anniversary of the Japanese government postal service. The standing figure of Baron Mitsu Mayejima is just the slightest degree less formal than the truncated head of the Prince of Liechtenstein, but that the two designs, Japanese and Liechtensteiner, are "out of the same stable" will be apparent even to those without the least knowledge of art. The identity of artistic conception will be obvious to all who see the two designs.

*   *   *

That, in the history of art, development of execution has gone hand in hand with, and has been dependent upon, development of the tools with which the artist works and the materials upon which he works, is a truism which needs only to be mentioned, and not to be elaborated upon, here.

It is mentioned here, of course, to note that changes in stamp-design have always been conditioned by the various new techniques in printing which have been introduced since the Uniform Penny Postage Act was passed by the two Houses of Parliament and received the Royal Assent.

Steel-engraving, embossing, surface-printing, typography, printing from hand-set type, lithography, recess-printing, electrotype, rotogravure and the various methods of photogravure—all these methods of reproducing the artist's original work have been used, during the just-over one hundred years since the first postage stamp was printed off engraved steel plates by Messrs. Perkins, Bacon & Petch. But of all the methods of reproduction none has effected so complete a change as the photographic method, first used—so far as the writers have discovered—in the "offset-printed" issue of Bavaria, 1914, whose astonishingly "modern" look is due simply to the fact that the method used in printing has since been almost universally adopted.

It is a singular fact that the "half-tone" process of reproducing pictures—no matter whether they be drawings or photographs—was certainly invented before 1827, for it was in that year that the man who claimed to have invented the process published a work on his method. A process of photographing direct on to the prepared wood block, so that the wood-engraver could then "work up" the block, was being used by some journals, notably the always-innovating *Illustrated London News*, as early as the time of the Crimean War; and it was this method of engraving which was used to prepare the earlier "pictorials", which were prepared from photographs.

By the end of the nineteenth century the half-tone process (which, by the way, is the process used to provide the illustrations to this book) had been sufficiently developed to have pretty well superseded older methods of reproducing drawings; and, in addition, the half-tone process made it possible to illustrate magazines, newspapers and books with photographs.

The advantage of reproducing an artist's work by photography is that the design may be transferred from the original sketch so that the original drawing or painting may be reproduced direct, without the necessity of its being re-drawn by the engraver. Thus the reproduced work is identical with the artist's original drawing.

Again, by dispensing, in the reproduction, not only with the engraver but with the work of engraving, the photographic—or half-tone—method enables the "shaded" effects to be reproduced with absolute fidelity. (In passing, it may be mentioned that both engraving and half-tone reproduce the picture by means of tiny incisions in the metal plate—copper or steel—from which the prints are taken; but in engraving the incisions are made by the engraver's "burin", with which he cuts into the metal, while with the half-tone method the

11

"black" parts of the picture are bitten out of the metal, in a mass of tiny dots, by the action of an acid. The engraved stamp, examined under a powerful magnifying-glass, is seen to be built up of somewhat bold—and deep—lines and dots, while the photographically reproduced stamp is seen to be built up of a mass of tiny, equal-sized dots, whose dimensions depend upon the size of the "screen" used in the reproduction.)

The photographic methods of reproduction opened up an entirely new field in philatelic art. Not only could the artist draw or paint his designs in the full confidence that they would be accurately reproduced; but he was no longer limited to drawing in "line" or "stipple". To use a non-technical phrase, he could "shade" as much as he liked, knowing that the photographic method of reproduction would accurately transfer his original drawing or painting to the stamp.

The comparison between the results of the new and an older method of reproduction may be well seen by comparing the first stamp produced by the new method—the Bavaria 1914—with a stamp issued only three years before by the same state—the 1911 series, issued in connection with the birthday and the jubilee of the Prince Regent of Bavaria.

This 1911 series—there are three types of stamps in what was technically two issues (though in the same year)—comprise some extremely handsome stamps; but it is easy to see how the photographic method used in the 1914 issue gives a softness of texture to the picture quite absent from the engraved reproductions of the 1911 issues.

Again, inevitably, the half-tone method enables the stamp to bear a direct photograph, such, for instance as was carried by the Belgian Congo issue of 1934, commemorating the death of King Albert I. Belgium, the home-country, had in fact used a photographically reproduced head of King Albert earlier—on the 75c. brown and 1f. lake of the 1931 issue— but the photographic block had been slightly "worked up" by the engraver who had prepared the engraved frame. On the other hand, the stamp issued to commemorate the tragic death of the young Queen Astrid, in 1935, is a true photograph, as were the earlier issues of 1934 (King Leopold III) and 1935 (The Royal Children: "Queen's Appeal" issue).

The advantage of the photographic methods of stamp-production, from a government point of view, is that money is saved. With earlier methods it was necessary to have an artist to make the preliminary sketch, an engraver to transfer the sketch to the plate, and the printer to print-off the stamps from the plate. By photography, the artist's drawing is transferred direct to the plate, so that the engraver is cut out, with a corresponding saving of his fees.

It follows, then, that those countries which have relied rather more than have others on the revenue-producing qualities of their stamps have taken wholeheartedly to the photographic methods of stamp-production, both because those methods are cheaper than older methods, and because, by the photographic methods, stamps of a meretricious and eye-catching splendour may be produced at a fraction of the cost of a plain stamp made by the older means.

Soviet Russia, de Gaulle France, Bulgaria, Czechoslovakia, Hitler Germany and so forth, to say nothing of Mussolini's Italy, have taken with enthusiasm to the photographic stamp; though this does not mean to say that more "solid" states, such as the United States and Great Britain, have neglected the opportunities offered by the half-tone method of stamp-production.

There is one disadvantage in the method, however, which has already caused a reaction, not so much against the method of reproduction, as against the temptation—knowing that anything may be reproduced—to reproduce anything. The photographically reproduced stamps—with the notable exceptions of such issues as those of King Edward VIII and certain issues of Hitler Germany and Pétain France—tended to be overcrowded with both subject and *action*. Too much subject: the 1,000f. French air-stamp of 1950, showing a strangely discrete City of Paris; or the Ethiopian air-stamp of the same year, showing the U.P.U. monument at Berne, the Emperor's head (in a cloud) and some mixed French and Amharic lettering which disturbs, without completing, the total design.

Too much action: the Bulgarian issue of 1939, especially the 5l. value, showing an express delivery van; the 1941 U.S. air-stamp, showing a twin-engined mail-plane; and the 1933 issue of Italy, in connection with the fiftieth anniversary of the foundation of the Eritrean colony—from which designs it would seem that the 1894 U.S. issue was not entirely free from Italian influence.

The reaction has been towards an almost childlike (not yet *childish*, be it noted!) simplicity. And here, in the search for simplicity, a curious result is apparent: by the new methods of reproduction designs are being printed which owe their inspiration to styles whose simplicity was conditioned by the relative difficulties of the older methods of reproduction.

In other words, the plain designs of the eighteen-forties and the eighteen-fifties are—suitably modified—now coming out again, subtly improved by the richer coloration that the new photographic methods (rotogravure, offset, etc.) make possible.

In this new plain style some of the British Commonwealth countries are showing an admirable example that the home country has yet to copy. While the stamps of Great Britain— especially the various commemoratives which have appeared since 1935 (Pl. XV)—have shown a regrettable tendency to be fussy, with excellently designed details incongruously put together, some Commonwealth issues have been admirable for an understanding both of the possibilities and the limitations of the photographic-reproduction methods.

Nothing, for instance, could be more tasteful than the Malta issue, commemorating the visit of the present Queen, when she was Princess Elizabeth (Pl. X). This is a straightforward photograph, "touched up" with the engraver's tool; but the care and good taste with which the royal cypher, the numeral, the George Cross and the word "Malta" are disposed about the portrait make this issue a classic among modern stamps.

There is another danger in the careless use of the photographic method of stamp-production: a danger which has not gone unnoticed by some governments. This is the tendency of the method to make for an at least superficial sameness,

so that, at first glance, some issues of Soviet Russia, the
United States, Netherlands Indies and many other governments would seem to have been not only ordered from the
same printers but drawn by the same artist.

The national characteristic, expressed in art, was always
present in the old days: hideous as they were, the later stamps
of Queen Victoria were still unmistakably British. It would
be hard to claim an equal "Britishness" for, say, Mr. Barnett
Freedman's Silver Jubilee design of 1935 (Pl. XV). Nor is there
anything more unmistakably British about the design for the
1947 Royal Visit stamps of Southern Rhodesia.

The fact is this: that, not only did not two engravers
reproduce a design in exactly the same way, the same engraver
did not reproduce a design twice in exactly the same way,
whereas the camera will make an infinite number of precisely
identical reproductions. Thus, when all stamps had either to
be engraved or lithographed, there was an individuality about
its execution which is missing in the half-tone reproductions
of to-day, even where these do reproduce an artist's work and
are not merely photographs.

It is not easy to explain why this should be so, since the
methods of reproduction should not obscure artistic differences;
but the fact is that there does seem to be a power resident
in the new reproduction methods to make the work of artists
tend to a universal sameness.

Fortunately there are signs that the danger has been seen
—perhaps by the governments who commission artists, perhaps by the artists themselves. Certainly, the new issue of
the Portuguese colony of Mocambique, of tropical birds on a
brilliant monochrome background, showed a marked desire
on the part of the artist to break fresh ground in design; and
his initiative is not lessened by the fact that the new Netherlands "Summer Flowers" issue of 1952 owes a great deal
either to the originator of the new Mocambique issue or to
the source of the latter's inspiration.

All in all, there seems to be apparent a desire to return to
national characteristic in philatelic art; a desire, perhaps not
yet fully realised, to equate the "Iron Curtain" philosophies

with a love of material products—skyscrapers, hydro-electric dams, underground railways, aeroplanes, and so on—and the philosophies of those countries of what has come to be called "the West" with an equally characteristic love of natural riches—trees and rocks and flowers and brilliantly coloured birds.

Once again we see symbolism being affected by politics, and art being affected by symbolism.

There is one point, though, which must be made: the art of the postage stamp has long been governed by its own rules; and often these rules run completely counter to the most cherished prejudices of the nations whose governments commission the stamps' designs.

To take one example of this artistic independence of social convention: the strictest of Moslem creeds, Islam, of course forbids the representation of any living object; and dislikes the representation (so as to be on the—theologically—safe side) even of inanimate objects.

Yet even so "puritan" a Moslem state as Saudi Arabia permitted, on its 1936 Charity (Medical Aid) issue, a drawing of the General Hospital at Mecca, while since that date other pictorial designs have appeared. Nor is this "plenary absolution" from the strict rules of theological convention a new thing. The old Ottoman Empire issued a pictorial series as early as 1913, while the portrait of the Sultan Mohammed V was shown on a series of 1916.

In fact, *all* the Moslem states—even to the very small ones, such as Bahawalpur, on the stamps of which appears not only the head of the Ameer, but also the U.P.U. monument at Berne (this piece of modern baroque including, of course, some classically underdressed female figures!)—use, or have used, those representations of nature which, in the strict Moslem view, are forbidden to the Believer.

Again, there is noticeable in the designs which emanate from non-Western countries a decidedly "western" sentiment, almost as though, because the first stamp emanated from the West, all stamps, even those from Oriental lands, should, more or less, exhibit a Western "feeling", both in

general design and in the details of that design, to say nothing
of the technique of production.

It is true, of course, that certain early issues of Oriental
Middle Asiatic countries were artistically characteristic of the
lands and peoples that they were meant to serve, and that
the Western aspect of succeeding issues was due to the fact
that the more "sophisticated" issues were designed in London
or Paris or New York. And again, there can be no denying
the influence on the issues of the Chinese Empire of the earlier
issues of those Great Powers whose treaty ports thrived on
the Chinese mainland.

All the same, though China and Japan and Afghanistan
and Thibet have endeavoured, at various times, to strike a
purely national note in their stamp issues, all have ended up
by producing stamp issues which are as Western as, say, those
of Hungary or Czechoslovakia.

It is interesting, then, in this connection to note that the
recent issues of South Korea—a state which owes its very
existence to Western arms—exhibit a strikingly Oriental
"feeling" in design.

Indeed, of the 100-wn. value of the 1951 issue only the value
in Arabic numerals and the words "Korea" in Roman letters
are "Western" details: all the rest, both in detail and general
conception, is as characteristically non-Western as, say, the
1881 issue of Nepal or the 1916 issue of Hedjaz.

But, as a rule, the Western influence is strikingly present,
no matter where the stamps originate. All portraits, for instance, are drawn (where they are not photographed) according
to a Western convention, and with the growth of photography
the Western touch must survive in even greater strength,
since Western art, at the time of the Renascence, adopted the
photographic perspective.

What, then, do the indications show for the stamp-fashions
of the future? Well, there will always be a harking back to
older modes, such as happened with the 1947 air-stamp issue
of Costa Rica or the 5c. stamp of the Cuba issue of 1942—
stamps which could have been designed fifty years earlier.
and, as happened with the 1919 Peace Celebration issue of

Switzerland, some stamps will be in advance of the general taste.

But the writers do see a general tendency to simplicity: a simplicity forced on the world's governments by the really general abuse of the stamp's illustrative power, so that the small space available has been too often crowded out, and the message of the stamp has been rendered meaningless by a sheer swamping.

Again, where every nation may boast some hydro-electric dam, some giant aeroplane, some presidential palace—looking like every other presidential palace in the world—there will be no point in sending out photographic studies of these marvels; and so governments will revert to the earlier idea of the stamp which had to indicate plainly only its source and its value.

Such a stamp is the design for the 1945 War Relief Fund of Switzerland, or that for the 1937 issue of Lithuania. The designs for the third of the three 1950 issues of Portuguese Timor belong to the same modest, unequivocal class.

There will always be a future for philatelic art, as there is a past; but it seems to the writers that the tendency of future stamp-design will be to seek its inspiration in the very earliest —the simpler—productions of the philatelic-artist, and not in the productions of that more florid middle-period out of which, it would appear, we are just emerging.

Index